D1824043

Perspectives in European History

No. 19

CHATHAM'S COLONIAL POLICY

CHATHAM'S COLONIAL POLICY

A STUDY IN THE FISCAL AND ECONOMIC IMPLICATIONS OF THE COLONIAL POLICY OF THE : : ELDER PITT : :

BY

KATE HOTBLACK, B.A., F.R.HIST.S.

J. E. CAIRNES SCHOLAR OF GIRTON COLLEGE, 1913-1915

"When trade is at stake, it is your last entrenchment—you must defend it or perish."

—From PITT'S SPEECH ON THE CONVENTION.

PORCUPINE PRESS

Philadelphia

First edition 1917
(London: George Routledge & Sons, Ltd., 1917)

Reprinted 1980 by
PORCUPINE PRESS INC.
Philadelphia, PA 19107

Library of Congress Cataloging in Publication Data

Hotblack, Kate.
    Chatham's colonial policy.

    (Perspectives in European history ; no. 19)
    Reprint of the 1917 ed. published by G. Routledge,
London, and Dutton, New York.
      1. Pitt, William, 1st Earl of Chatham, 1708-1778.
2. Great Britain—Colonies. 3. Great Britain—Com-
mercial policy. 4. Statesmen—Great Britain—
Biography.   I. Title.
DA483.P6H6   354.41061′092′4   80-21263
ISBN 0-87991-626-5

Manufactured in the United States of America

CONTENTS

APPENDIX

ix

PREFACE

I wish to express my gratitude to the authorities of Girton College, Cambridge, for enabling me to make the researches for this study, in connexion with the J. E. Cairnes Scholarship (1913-1915). My thanks are also due to His Grace the Duke of Bedford, K.G., for permission to consult the Woburn Manuscripts ; to Mr. Hubert Hall, of His Majesty's Public Record Office, and to Mr. Harold Temperley, Fellow of Peterhouse, Cambridge (now Captain in the Fife and Forfar Yeomanry), for generous help ; also to Mrs. O. S. Watkins, who kindly read my proof-sheets. For the defects of this little book I alone am responsible.

K. H.

INTRODUCTION

" It was the fashion to say that Mr. Pitt was violent, impetuous, romantick, a despisor of money, intrigue and patronage, ignorant of the characters of men, and one who disregarded consequences. Nothing can be less just than the whole of this, which may be judged by the leading features of his life without relying on any private testimony.

· · · · · ·

" There is no describing the pains and consideration he gave to the minutest action." [1]—Shelburne.

THE acid of Shelburne's etching has bitten deep, but true and modern historians have closely followed the lines which the contemporary traced with such bitter precision. The story of the struggles of Pitt's early years, the connections he made, and his schooling in Cobham's Cubbery is Lord Rosebery's contribution to that Life of Chatham which he declares can never be written. Dr. von Ruville has told us more than enough of the influence of money upon the life of the man whose public honesty appalled the King of Sardinia, and whose generous carelessness in his private affairs nearly drove his faithful solicitor Nutall to distraction. Mr. Frederic Harrison was one of the first to vouch for the sanity of Pitt's statesmanship ; and Mr. Hubert Hall's essays on Chatham's colonial policy prove the coherence of his imperial design. Pitt was practical, he did not despise money ; he was involved in intrigue during the whole of his political career ; he refused office without patronage, knowing it to be worthless ; and from his intimate knowledge of the characters of men he was able to foretell the results of more than one political event.

---

[1] Fitzmaurice's " Life of Shelburne," vol. i., pp. 75 and 76.

Nor is Shelburne's other dictum less true. Pitt was a worker who gave infinite pains and consideration to the minutest action. This fact is often overlooked. Pitt's genius dazzled the eyes of contemporaries, and posterity has been slow to realise that it was but the torch by whose aid he explored the obscure track of statecraft.[1] The complexity of Chatham's character and the apparent artificiality of the times in which he lived baffle while they attract, and have hitherto rendered any continuous study of his policy extraordinarily difficult.[2] The Great Commoner long remained as inscrutable as he would have desired, but Mr. Basil Williams' " Life of William Pitt " has given us a living Chatham. His statesmanship also can now be tested by the only useful standard—that of his own time. During the last ten years enormous advances have been made in our knowledge of the eighteenth century. Mr. Temperley and Mr. Winstanley have discovered the cabinet system of the early Hanoverians; and Professor Andrews, Dr. Beer, and other American scholars have begun the scientific study of the effects of mercantilism upon the transatlantic colonies. The Cabinet Councils of George II were the scenes of Pitt's intrigues and dominion; those of George III witnessed his downfall. To secure the commerce of the New World for the English-speaking peoples was the main object of his ambition. A clearer knowledge of the conditions under which the Great Commoner was forced to work and a better understanding of the nature of the prize for which he strove are incalculable aids to the study of his colonial policy.

Probably to Pitt himself his work appeared the greatest thing in his life. He consciously fitted himself for this great task, fought fiercely for the power

---

[1] Cf. Basil Williams' " Life of William Pitt."
[2] Cf. Lord Rosebery's " Chatham," p. vii.

to enter upon it, and, when the opportunity came, acted with the decision of forethought. As early as 1736 the *Craftsman* had commented on Pitt's close study of foreign affairs. During the War of Jenkins' Ear the budding statesman was able to apply his theories in criticism of the policy of older politicians. Here he blundered half consciously through the spirit of opposition that he chose to assume, half—as he himself afterwards declared—through ignorance. Pitt learned much at this time. Not only did he criticise his political opponents at home ; he marked down for future use the strength and weakness of the enemy. Among his papers are several lists of notes made in 1742 which deal with the Spanish colonies. There is also a careful estimate of the French national revenue for the same year.[1] Whilst in subordinate office as Paymaster-General, Pitt was consulted upon American affairs both by Newcastle[2] and Bedford[3] ; and after the failure of Braddock's ill-fated expedition there were those who remembered that Mr. Pitt had been one of the first to point out the inadequacy of the preparations.[4] Pitt's colonial policy was the result of many years' careful study ; the brilliant strategy of the Seven Years' War had been sketched in outline long before. When he said, " I can save this country," he knew how he was going to do it. And if in 1756 Pitt founded his boasts on knowledge which during the next four years stood the test of trial by battle, a decade later he spoke with the authority of an expert. It is one of the objects of this thesis to show how he achieved this position.

As Secretary of State during the Seven Years' War Pitt had unrivalled opportunities for studying the economic conditions of the American colonies and their commercial relations with the Mother Country.

---

[1] Chatham Papers.
[3] Bedford Corr., vol. i., p. 34.
[2] Addit. MSS. 32721.
[4] Addit. MSS. 35909.

From 1757 till 1760, the period of his personal supremacy, Pitt's jealous colleagues declared that the whole war was the plan of one man : but for a plan which included the capture of Quebec and the expedition to Martinique criticism would have been as futile as a purely formal sanction. Pitt's war plans give us the outline of his imperial design ; the terms of peace that he proposed or sanctioned supply further details ; but the clearest exposition both of Pitt's plans and the methods by which he executed them is to be found in his destructive criticism of the treaty that his opponents negociated after his resignation. There is hardly a line of this magnificent oration which could not be proved from the state papers on which indeed it was based. It was one of the occasions on which Pitt spoke with authority, and his eloquence gained the laboriously acquired simplicity of true art.

At the greatest crisis in the history of the English-speaking peoples Chatham spoke still more clearly ; and again his appeal was more to men's reason than their passions. The Great Commoner's instinctive love of liberty and fair play illuminates his speeches ; but he also urged moderation from prosaic commercial considerations. He reminded Englishmen of the value of the trade that might be lost if they drove the Americans to desperation ; for Chatham predicted that in such a struggle the colonists would be successful. Later he approved, and indeed partly composed, Shelburne's speech on the Repeal of the Stamp Act, a speech in which the President of the Board of Trade dealt almost entirely with the commercial view of the question, and displayed an intimate knowledge of the colonial point of view.[1] The American colonists regarded Pitt as " a man of peculiar discernment," and one of the few English statesmen who understood colonial affairs. Pitt's correspondence with the

---

[1] Addit. MSS. 35912, ff. 76 ; see *American Historical Review*, April, 1912.

Admiralty and the Board of Trade tells the same tale. Even in his most extravagant and purely party speeches, from 1738 onwards, a line of policy may be traced. The means employed by Pitt were many, his words often contradictory ; but his method of reasoning and his aims were always the same. He designed an Empire for Great Britain, and that empire was to be one of trade rather than of territory.

TO

J. H.

CHATHAM'S COLONIAL POLICY

CHAPTER I

PITT AND THE WAR OF JENKINS' EAR

"When trade is at stake, it is your last entrenchment—you must defend it or perish."

—From Pitt's Speech on the Convention.

THE Convention of 1739, Pitt's first great lesson in the importance of trade in connection with foreign policy, was an honest attempt on the part of Walpole and the peace party to settle the long-standing dispute with Spain about our trade with the West Indies and the Right of Search. The real difficulty lay in the artificial system of international trade regulations at this date, the cause of most of the great wars of the eighteenth century. It was a recognised principle with eighteenth-century economists that the colony existed for the commercial good of the mother country, a good interpreted by the crude mercantilist dictum, "You are to take our manufactures and supply us with raw products, and if possible naval stores." Each colony was considered as "a choice branch springing from the main root." It was the duty of the parent state to give nourishment to its offshoot; but no project for the good of the colony was to be considered on its own merits, but only so far as it contributed towards the general balance of the whole state. In fact, the colony was to be "a useful and profitable

I   B

member." [1] The ideal was imperial as well as commercial, or rather from an eighteenth-century standpoint the two things meant the same. Commerce
was the tie which bound the colony to the parent
state, perhaps the only bond possible in an age of slow
communications and corrupt political organisation.

For these reasons illicit trade between a colony and
a foreign state, or between the colonies of different
states, was a serious offence, the action of an ungrateful
child, a blow at imperial unity, a drain on the national
resources. Colonial Governors declared that if illicit
trade were not checked in the American colonies it
would loose them from their allegiance to Great
Britain ; [2] and English statesmen, fearing the loss of
the American trade, said, " What then will become of
us ? " [3]

The colonial point of view is not so clear ; nor is
it possible to generalise on a subject where the evidence
is so conflicting. England was not a bad centre for
the enumerated commodities which the colonies
could only sell to her. There are also the questions
of bounties and drawbacks to be considered, and the
encouragement the mother country gave to colonial
timber and tobacco. [4] Yet it is plain that, even where
the actual monetary loss to the colony was slight, the
restrictions were irksome.

But in the case of the Spanish colonies the hardship
was material as well as sentimental. Spain was a poor
shopkeeper, and her colonies, finding they could not
get supplied from the home stores, went elsewhere. [5]

---

[1] King's MSS., Brit. Mus. 205, f. 46. Copy of an address of Sir
William Keith, Knight, sometime Deputy-Governor of Pennsylvania,
to the King, 1728.

[2] Coll. Corr.

[3] *American Historical Review*, April, 1912.

[4] *Cf.* Cunningham, " History of English Industry and Commerce,
Modern Times," part i., p. 588.

[5] " The Theory and Practice of Commerce and Maritime Affairs,"
by Don Geronymo de Uztariz, translated by John Kippax, 1751,
vol. i., p. 159.

Spanish custom-house officials connived at the importation of English goods ; and so great were the profits to be gained by trading with the Spanish colonies that Englishmen were willing to risk even the loss of their ears. Where the advantage is large enough men will always be found to risk life and limb ; and when a law is in opposition to the will of the whole people, it will always be broken. These maxims are trite enough now ; but they were very imperfectly understood in the eighteenth century ; nor do they alone give a satisfactory explanation of the position of 1739. That can only be understood when regarded as an acute stage in the history of Anglo-Spanish trade.

The Spaniards began their American policy by simply claiming the whole of the New World. They had found it, they declared, and their annexation had been blessed and confirmed by the Pope, a notable factor in international law, the arbiter of many a dispute in the Middle Ages. But though first in the field, the Spaniards were centuries too late for the policy they tried to pursue. In an age when the temporal power of the Church was largely discredited, people cared little about the bull of Alexander VI, and in the sixteenth century Spain was forced to acknowledge the established fact of the Portuguese colony of Brazil. After he had annexed Portugal, Philip II tried to repress the growing colonial power of Great Britain. The Armada settled the fate of the New World as well as of the old. Elizabeth viewed the Spanish gold mines with envious eyes ; and the piratical expeditions of Drake, Hawkins, and a crowd of lesser men did much to embitter the relations between England and Spain. One could not " singe the King of Spain's beard " with impunity. The Armada settled the fate of the New World as well as of the old.

The seventeenth century left Spanish America in a sad plight, drained by the exertions of Philip II ;

the vigour of Spain continued to decrease; the expulsion of Protestants meant the emigration of wealth.
Population, manufactures, fleets, and foreign commerce declined in succession.   Soon the needs of her
colonies far exceeded the supplies of the mother
country. The result was a huge contraband trade,
which in its turn encouraged the aggressive policy
of England, France, and Holland. The English, under
Cromwell, had even hoped to capture Havana, the
back door of the treasure-house of Spain; they had
actually succeeded in the capture of Jamaica, thus
pushing in a wedge into that crescent of islands that
guards the Gulf of Mexico.

Unable to supply her own colonists, Spain partly
legalised the trade of other nations by the system of
granting licences to foreign ships. The Anglo-Spanish
commercial treaty of 1670 secured a certain liberty
of navigation to Great Britain, who in return admitted
the much-debated Spanish right of search. But this
was specially stated to apply only to search for arms,
ammunition, and soldiers.[1] Spain also tried to meet the
demands of her colonies by taking a trading partner.
She had little to export, and was forced to fill her
outward-bound galleons with the manufactures of
England, France, and Holland. Two results followed:
the powers of Europe all aimed at becoming the
favoured nation of Spanish commercial treaties; and
the treasure of New Spain no longer belonged to the
mother country, anticipated before it reached Cadiz,
the return cargo went to enrich the country whose
exports had paid for it.[2]

The War of the Spanish Succession brought about
many commercial changes; an influx of French
bullion helped to restore the Spanish finances, and the
Treaty of Utrecht contained the famous Assiento

---

[1] Coxe's " Walpole," vol. i., p. 557.
[2] Robertson, " History of America," vol. ii., p. 403 ; Clarke,
" Letters from Spain, 1760."

clause which gave England the right to send an annual trading ship to Spanish America. The Assiento ship legalised part of the English trade with the Spanish colonies, and increased the traders' knowledge of the colonists' needs. The abuse of the privilege was notorious. The Spaniards complained that this one ship was equivalent to more than five or six of the largest galleons. For we are told that :

"Whilst the English were permitted to send an annual ship, called *navio de permisso*, she used to bring to the fair a very large cargo on her own account, never failing first to touch at Jamaica, so that her loading alone was more than half of all those brought by the galleons ; for besides that her burthen so far exceeded five hundred Spanish tuns, that it was even more than nine hundred ; she had no provisions, water, or other things, which fill a great part of the hold ; she indeed took them in at Jamaica, from whence she was attended by five or six smaller vessels loaded with goods, which when they arrived near Porto Bello were put on board her, and the provisions removed into tenders ; by which artifice that single ship was made to carry more than five or six of the largest galleons ; and this nation having a free trade, and selling cheaper than the Spaniards, that indulgence was of infinite detriment to the commerce of Spain." [1]

Besides the abuse of the Assiento ship, there was a large illicit trade between New England and New Spain. Jamaica was the depôt of another branch of this lucrative traffic. So well was the position of affairs understood in England, that one of the declared objects of the foundation of Georgia was to carry on a trade with the Spanish colonies in Central America ; for, a memorialist says :

---

[1] " A Voyage to South America (1735), undertaken by Command of his Majesty the King of Spain." By Don Juan and Don Antonio de Ulloa. Both captains of the Spanish Navy, members of the Royal Societies of London and Berlin, vol. i., p. 107.

" Let our neighbours lay what prohibitions or restraints they please on their subjects in those parts. Experience proves that where the cheapness of goods recommend them, their introduction cannot be prevented." [1]

In 1739 it was computed that England had as large a share in Spanish colonial trade in ways prohibited as the Spaniards themselves had in authorised ways. Indeed, the Spanish galleons are said to have fallen two years before from 15,000 to 2,000 tons.[2] It became clear that Spain had failed to meet the demands of her colonies and that other nations had stepped in. The situation, which was a grave one in a century when commercial monopoly was the leading principle of all intercourse between parent state and colony, was rendered still worse by the regulations under which Spain governed her trade. This was in the hands of a few great houses which made enormous profits, a hundred, two hundred, sometimes even three hundred per cent., the ideal of the Spanish trader being high prices and small markets.[3]

During the first half of the eighteenth century Spain carried on her American trade by annual expeditions of three kinds—the flota, the register ships, and the galleons.[4] The flota was a fleet of three men of war, and fourteen or fifteen merchant ships from four hundred to five thousand tons burthen. It started from Cadiz and sailed straight to La Vera Cruz, where it landed its European cargo, and in exchange took one of plate, precious stones, cochineal, indigo, cocoa, tobacco, sugar, and hides. From La Vera Cruz the flota sailed to Havana, which was the rendezvous where they met the galleons. The galleons

---

[1] Addit. MSS. 35905, f. 72.
[2] Robertson, vol. ii., p. 409.
[3] *Ibid.*, vol. ii., p. 403.
[4] A graphic description of Spanish trade is to be found in the letters of Edward Clarke, chaplain to the British ambassador at Madrid, 1760-1761. His observations are confirmed by Ulloa and Uztariz.

formed another fleet, which carried on the trade with Terra Firma by Cartagena and Peru, and by Panama and Portobello. They consisted of eight men of war, and were originally designed to supply Peru with military stores, but, a contemporary writer says, " in reality were loaded with every kind of merchandise on a private account, so as to be in too weak a condition either to defend themselves or to attack others." [1] Under their convoy they had twelve sail of merchant ships of about the same burthen. News of the arrival of the fleet was sent to Panama and the chief neighbouring towns. Then for a fortnight Portobello was the scene of a great fair, where gold, silver, and precious stones were bartered for the best of European manufactured goods. Fabulous tales were told of the great fair at Portobello. Spanish sailors declared that they had seen ingots piled in heaps, and that wedges of pure gold were thrown about the wharves as things of little value.

The third expedition was that of the register ships ; these were of the nature of private ventures. Merchants received licences from the Council of the Indies to send ships of 300 tons to specified ports in the West Indies. The galleons and register ships met the flota at Havana. News was sent to Spain by some of the fastest sailing vessels that the treasure fleet was ready to return, and a convoy was despatched to protect them on the homeward journey.

The Spanish galleons which sailed from Havana carried some of the riches of both the Indies, for as Spain traded with South America, so South America traded with the Philippines and the far East. In July a great galleon set out from Manilla richly laden. In December she arrived at Acapulco, where another great fair was held which sometimes lasted thirty days. Many of the East India goods brought to

---

[1] Clarke, " Letters from Spain."

Acapulco from the Philippines and China were carried on trucks to Mexico ; some passed on to La Vera Cruz and the Islands, but most of the treasure was stored in the city till it could be exported to old Spain. Mexico was a place of the first importance, the channel of all the trade carried on between America and Europe on the one hand, and the East Indies on the other.

Such an ostentatious stream of gold and rich merchandise excited the envy of all Europe. As early as 1720 it was debated in England whether Gibraltar might not be bartered to Spain for twice its worth in commerce. To gain a legal share in the Spanish trade was the object of both Walpole and Pitt, but they differed violently as to the means by which the desired end was to be attained. Walpole hoped for peace because he feared war. While he negotiated with Spain he kept a watchful eye on the court at Versailles, and listened anxiously for rumours from Vienna. For in 1739 all Europe was waiting for Charles VI to die. Walpole foresaw that the Emperor's death would be followed by a great war. He hoped by the convention to settle our disputes with Spain, and make her our ally before the great storm which was threatening broke over Europe. He was willing to make an easy settlement because he believed that our trade with the Spanish West Indies was illegal, and hoped that a treaty of commerce might follow the Anglo-Spanish alliance. Above all, he feared the union of France and Spain, whom he knew to be already partners in trade.[1]

Pitt represented a large party both within and without the House. He thought that we could gain the Spanish trade more easily by war than by peace. The trade had been carried on so long with impunity that England had come to look upon it as legalised by custom. The right of search was as intolerable

---

[1] Coxe's " Walpole," vol. i., p. 603.

to Englishmen as their infringements of international trade regulations were to Spain. There is little doubt that the violence of Pitt's speeches was a party pose ; but it was a good day for Great Britain when the future Secretary of State was forced to consider the strategic value of the West Indies. Walpole held the key to the situation, but he thought it was a key which, like Bluebeard's, it was as well not to fit into the lock. This lock was to be found at Havana, which Oliver Cromwell had called the gate of the treasure-house of Spain ; for Havana commanded the Gulf of Mexico, where the riches of East and West met and were exchanged.

Pitt violently attacked the convention and the " fatal influence that framed it." Yet, though the weapon with which he attacked Walpole was covered with a transparent sheath of sarcasm, the steel beneath rang true. The point of his attack was his real grasp of the situation. The young orator tried to break down his opponent's guard with irony. " To what are gentlemen reduced in support of it ? First try a little to defend it upon its merits ; if that is not tenable, throw out general terrors the House of Bourbon is united." Then suddenly he thrust home : " Who knows the consequence of a war ? Sir, Spain knows the consequence of a war in America ; whoever gains it must prove fatal to her, she knows it and must therefore avoid it ; but she knows England does not dare to make it, and what is a delay which is all this magnificent convention is sometimes called to produce ? " Here is the same line of reasoning, the same policy he rightly urged in 1761. Spain, weak but proud and aggressive, must be brought to reason before her power equalled her pretensions.

The war which followed in 1739 was ineffectual. The plan for an attack upon Havana was not executed. The capture of Portobello only succeeded in adding Hosiers' ghost to Walpole's political opponents. Pitt

himself, in 1757, so far imitated the convention policy
as to try to gain a share of the Spanish trade by peaceful methods.   He even proposed to sacrifice Gibraltar ;
but he failed in 1757, as Walpole had failed in 1739,
and was driven to return to his first policy of war as a
means of making trade flourish.

In 1739 Pitt's commercial policy was still in the
making; what he had grasped was that we had been
pursuing a lucrative trade which was now threatened.
Spain was beginning to give a belated attention to
commerce, and endeavouring to stop our illicit trade
by searching English ships who sailed within her sphere
of influence.   This procedure, which was justified in
one sense by its success, was really a claim to Spanish
suzerainty over the Gulf of Mexico.   This in turn
involved a claim to naval supremacy which England
could not admit.   As Granville said, the Right of
Search was a thing that did not exist.   It is true that
in 1751 Pitt himself admitted that it was impossible
to cry, " No Search ; " he had by that time realised the
Spanish side of the question ; we were infringing her
trade regulations and aiding her colonies to break the
very laws which we stringently enforced in our own.
Yet in 1767 he again insisted that Spanish pretensions to
exclusive rights in certain waters should be withstood.[1]

Pitt's papers show how carefully he studied the
connection between commercial and foreign policy
during the War of Jenkins' Ear.   An estimate of the
French national revenue proves that as early as 1741
he saw how important it was to consider the wealth
of France, Spain's commercial ally and family friend.[2]
The years of opposition were not merely employed
in the noisy clamour of youth and faction : they were
the years of preparation in which the future statesman studied his craft.

---

[1] Cf. Pitt's speeches.   [2] Chatham Papers.

CHAPTER II

PITT AND THE CITY

"The eighteenth century . . . was essentially the age of classical ideals and inspirations, with all that that great word signified, simplicity, proportion, restraint, dignity.

"To borrow the jargon of the present day, our fore-fathers did not talk imperially or think imperially, but contented themselves with acting as citizens of a nation destined to rule the world."
—From the "Life of Lord Chancellor Hardwicke," by Philip C. Yorke, 1913.

To-day the city of London is one of the greatest markets of the world. In the eighteenth century its operations were much less extensive, but its importance was infinitely greater. Though the trade of London was small if tested by modern standards, the city had a localised corporate life which is lacking to-day, for it contained the homes as well as the counting-houses of its merchants. Visitors to London were impressed by the wide streets and substantial buildings, " chiefly inhabited by tradesmen whose houses and shops make a better appearance than commonly those do in any other city in Europe.[1] Wealthy merchants lived in " elegant squares," and hard by the town houses of many " persons of rank " were also to be found. The Holborn members of the Duke of Bedford's " gang " had a convenient meeting-place in Bloomsbury ; and it was but a step from the Strand to Newcastle House in Lincoln's Inn Fields.

---

[1] " The Ambulator, or the Stranger's Companion in a Tour round London." Printed by J. Bew. 1774.

Though the city fathers were drawn from all classes, and sometimes became followers of the great parliamentary leaders, they formed a distinct society of their own. The younger son of a peer might marry the daughter of his father's steward and trade successfully with her dowry. The penniless lad might still by industry and good fortune rise to a position of wealth and esteem ; and it was only when he became ostentatious that he was reminded that his sister had cried hot rolls until very lately. One Lord Mayor gave banquets whose magnificence recalled those of Henry VIII and astonished even the Judges ; another surprised a distinguished guest by urging him to wreak havoc among the pines, " for eat or not eat we must pay." [1] Some of the wealthiest citizens possessed land, and a few had considerable parliamentary influence ; [2] but many substantial merchants were unrepresented, and forced to fall back upon the right to petition when they desired the redress of their grievances. The political disability of its members gave the corporation strength. A contemporary cartoon represents His Majesty presenting the petitions of the Livery of the City of London to a youthful heir bent on kite-building ; but usually the stiff parchment rolls received more respectful treatment ; for then as now the city held the purse-strings. Stocks and shares and government policy reacted upon one another constantly ; [3] and in a time of stress who should open a subscription list if not His Worship the Lord Mayor ?

Throughout his political career Pitt was closely

---

[1] City Biography, 1800, and numerous references to Beckford, Trecothick, and other city worthies in Walpole's " Memoires of George II and George III."

[2] Cf. Chatham MSS. 40, James Hodges (The Town Clerk) to Pitt, March 14, 1759. " P.S.—The Lord Mayor of the City of London who is lately elected a member of parliament has many good properties, is independent and has great integrity. I wish when you see him in the House of Commons you would take some notice of him."

[3] Thorold Rogers, " History of Agriculture and Prices," vol. vii., pp. 769-776.

connected with the citizens of London. They were
the audience for whom his early opposition speeches
were planned; their firm financial support made the
policy of his first ministry a reality; and all through his
life they contributed to the stock of his unrivalled
knowledge of commercial and colonial affairs.[1] Although frequently overbearing and, as they declared,
insolent in his manner to the great lords whom he
counted as his equals in rank, the Great Commoner
almost invariably treated the men of commerce with
courtesy and consideration. A sense of conscious
superiority was soothing to an over-sensitive nature.
Pitt turned with relief from Newcastle's armed
neutrality and Bedford's grudging admiration to the
unwavering loyalty of men like William Beckford and
Thomas Hollis.

Beckford was a prominent member of a large class
of independent merchants who rallied round Pitt.
The son of a successful sugar-planter, his childhood
was spent in Jamaica. When about fourteen he was
sent to England and educated at Westminster, where
he formed a lasting friendship with Murray and
Johnson, clever boys who were to become eminent
men. At this time Beckford himself is said to have
shown considerable abilities for classical studies, but
in after years he often cut a ridiculous figure in the
House through his inability to express himself concisely.
Through the early death of his elder brother he became
one of the richest men of his day; and his influence
in the city corresponded to his wealth and character.
In 1747 he was first elected member for the city, an
honour which he considered well worth the £400 he
gave for paving the streets. His immense fortune
making him independent of the ministry, he was
frequently to be found among the opposition; and a
mutual antipathy to Hanoverian politics was the first

---

[1] *Cf.* Basil Williams, " Life of Pitt," vol. i., p. 289.

bond of union that connected his career with that of
the Great Commoner.

Pitt is said to have declared that there were but two
roads to power, Royal and National.[1] The first was
long barred to him ; and though in later years he
made good use of the King's highway when expedition
was essential, the path he loved best led across the
open spaces of the nation's common ground. His
first great speech appealed to an audience far larger
than that of Westminster. The Convention, he
declared, was " nothing but a stipulation for national
ignominy, an illusory expedient to baffle the resentment of the nation, a truce without a suspension of
hostilities on the part of Spain ; on the part of England a suspension of the first law of nature—self-
preservation and self-defence—a surrender of the
rights and trade of England to the mercy of pleni-
potentiaries, and in this infinitely highest and most
sacred part of future security not only inadequate,
but directly repugnant to the resolutions of Parliament and the promise from the throne." Such
sentiments called forth an echo at the street corners
of the city ; and the heads of great firms who sat snug
in the offices of their counting-houses applauded the
expression of a philosophy so congenial to their own.
The new men of an age which saw the birth of " the
rights of man " and the reincarnation of the law of
nature had found their chief. Later, when he thun-
dered against the continental diplomacy of the ministry,
Pitt began to gather round him an independent party,
formed of men like Beckford who were too rich to be
bought, and which had many adherents among the
unrepresented men of commerce. Pitt voiced their
grievances in the House, and in return they supplied
him with trustworthy information on commercial

---

[1] Phillimore's " Lyttleton," p. 453.

matters, which enabled him to single out the weak points of the government's economic policy.

As early as 1745 his opponents had learned to fear " Mr. Pitt's talents and efficiency,"[1] and tried to persuade the King to give him a responsible position in the ministry. But George II could not forgive the man who had championed the cause of his worthless heir and called Hanover a despicable electorate. It was only the calamities of an unguided war that forced him to submit to the dictation of William Pitt as the lesser evil.

Beckford was delighted when his friend was given the seals and the leadership of the House of Commons. He declared he had " a real good opinion of Mr. Pitt," but doubted whether his political influence was sufficient to give full scope to his great abilities.[2] Both hopes and fears were speedily confirmed. The Great Commoner drafted the King's speech before the session of 1757 so as to make it " captivating to the people."[3] George II insisted that the oration should be shortened. But even when shorn of some of its glowing periods the speech was national in a broad sense, for it took the people of England into the minister's confidence. They were told plainly that the settlement of the struggle for America was the great fundamental measure in view; and that this was to be supported by expeditions to the coast of Africa and to the East and West Indies.[4] The merchants recognised that the government was pledged to carry on a war for and upon trade, and determined that trade should support the war.[5] The refreshing shower of gold boxes that revived Pitt's drooping

---

[1] Addit. MSS. 32706, Chesterfield to Newcastle, Feb. 27, 1745.

[2] Chat. MSS. 19, Beckford to Cole, Dec. 13, 1756.

[3] Pitt to George II, Nov. 15, 1756 ; Torrens, vol. ii., p. 242.

[4] Cf. Basil Williams' " Pitt," and C. M. H., vol vi., p. 13, Dr. Wolfgang Michael.

[5] E.g. Chat. MSS. 17, James Auriol (a Lisbon merchant) to Pitt, Dec. 7, 1756, containing a scheme for raising supplies.

spirits during his short dismissal in 1757, like Peel's slender stock of Latin quotations, has long ago received its due meed of praise. When the Great Commoner returned to office he knew that the cities of England were with him, and was confident that with their aid he would eventually win the King's support.

In this time of trial, when the distrust of his Sovereign and the envy of his colleagues added much to the Secretary of State's burden, William Beckford was a firm and sympathetic supporter. On September 20, 1757, he wrote to Pitt, "I never longed for one success so much that the people might have one huzza."[1] And when victory came he was equally ready with genuine appreciation. On the day that the news of the success of the first African expedition reached England he declared : " Although the taking of Fort Louis may seem trifling, yet I am sure the commercial part of France will not look on it in that light, as there is now an end of all their commerce on the coast of Africa, a commerce more beneficial than any other in the known world."[2] How beneficial the African commerce was Beckford had good reason to know, for a contemporary accuses him and other leading city men of having advised the expedition solely in order to secure a convoy for their merchant ships.[3] But if self-interest was the ruling motive of city politicians, self-sacrifice also played its part in their support of the war. In the late summer of 1759, when all Pitt's argosies were ventured forth and suspense had become almost intolerable, the news of the reverse of our ally at Kunersdorf called forth Beckford's substantial sympathy. He worked hard in the city to raise a fresh loan, and took care that the notice of his own subscription of 100 guineas should appear

[1] Chat. MSS. 19, Beckford to Pitt, Sept. 20, 1757.
[2] Chatham Papers 19, Beckford to Pitt, June 12, 1758.
[3] Ibid. 53, Malachy Postlethwayt to Pitt, March 16, 1759.

in the *Gazette* the same day as the news of the defeat.[1]

But by that time Pitt was nearly at the zenith of his power. His own efficiency and the support of the city had secured him the use of the royal road to success. It was a maxim of eighteenth-century politics that though if a measure were submitted to the Cabinet Council the decision of the majority was the measure, yet a question of foreign policy might be decided by the King and his chief minister alone.[2] By 1758 George II had become convinced that it was necessary, at a time when the very existence of the state was threatened, to make William Pitt dictator. The power thus gained Pitt used relentlessly to put into speedy execution his plans for a war which should raise his nation " to as high pitch of prosperity and glory by unanimity at home—by confidence and reputation abroad—by alliances wisely chosen and faithfully observed—by colonies united and protected—by decisive victories by sea and land—by conquests made by arms and generosity in every part of the globe—and by commerce for the first time united with and made to flourish by war." [3]

Many of his expeditions were planned by the aid of advice received from merchants,[4] and in all he received the cordial support of commercial men both in the colonies and at home. The city raised supplies and

---

[1] Chatham Papers 19, Beckford to Pitt, Sept. 20, 1759.

[2] Addit. MSS. 35870, f. 310, and 32929, f. 18. Minutes of the Cabinet of Oct. 2. 1761. See Articles by Hunt and Temperley in *English Historical Review* for 1906.

[3] Burke's inscription on the monument in the Guildhall raised to the memory of William Pitt by the Mayor, Aldermen, and Common Council of the City of London.

[4] For the African Exped., see Chat. MSS. 20, Letters of Cumming to Pitt, and C.O. 276, 12 (Petition of Cumming to Pitt) ; also Chat. MSS. 53, Postlethwayt to Pitt, and Chat. MSS. 64, Thynne to Pitt. For American Exped., see Chat. MSS. 19, Dennys de Berdt to Pitt ; and Chat. MSS. 95, Petitions of Merchants trading to North America. For West Indies, see Chat. MSS. 19, Letters from Beckford, and 64, Gov. Thomas.

incidentally kept Pitt in office, for, when George II fretted at the restraints placed upon him by his self-imposed master, Newcastle " presumed to ask His Majesty whether he thought that this war, at this immense expense, could have been carried on without the unanimity of the people, the popularity of the Common Council, etc., which was entirely owing to Mr. Pitt, so that it could not have been done without him " ; to which argument the Duke received no reply.[1]

In return for his successes, Pitt received acclamation and advice from numerous merchants who were anxious as to the terms of peace which should result from such a war. One city father even compiled " A List of Successes and Miscarriages in the Last and Present War," and had it printed in an elegant manner, knowing that many persons would hang it in a frame to remind themselves and their children of the wonderful and uninterrupted exploits performed by our sea and land forces whilst Mr. Secretary Pitt ruled the Helm of Britain.[2]   On one point all Pitt's advisers were agreed—the French must be driven from North America, and the whole of the Newfoundland fishery secured to Great Britain.[3]

On other questions opinions were more divided. Beckford and some of the other leading West Indian merchants advised the conquest of Martinique solely in order to secure the price of Minorca.[4] This party feared that the retention of one of the considerable West Indian Islands would bring down the price of sugar, and prove injurious to the interests of our existing colonies.   Others more far-sighted urged that

---

[1] Yorke's " Life of Hardwicke," vol. iii., p. 73, Newcastle to Hardwicke, Oct. 25, 1759.

[2] Chat. MSS. 116, Sir Theodore Jannesen to Pitt, Northside, Soho Sq., Dec. 1, 1762.

[3] Chat. MSS. 19, Aug. 26, 1758, Beckford to Pitt. Chat. MSS. 53, Price to Pitt. Chat. MSS. 40, Hodges to Pitt.

[4] Chat. MSS. 19, Beckford to Pitt, Aug. 26, 1758.

some of our small islands were becoming exhausted, and that in any case they would soon be unable to meet the demands of our extended empire in North America.[1] Pitt adopted this latter view, experience was widening his vision. He never forgot that " the present war was undertaken for the long injured, long neglected, long forgotten people of America."[2] But neither did he abandon his early design for securing to Great Britain an empire of commerce. During his first ministry the crude ideas of his youth were developed and put to the test.

The accession of George III embarrassed both Pitt and the City. The former doubted the reception he would receive at Court and the support he might rely on in the Cabinet. The latter were torn between loyalty to the crown and attachment to the seals. When Pitt received back the Royal Speech for the opening of Parliament which he had submitted to the young king, he was horrified to find the war he had described as just and necessary stigmatised as bloody and expensive, and his references to our allies left out after the words expressing hope of a speedy peace. George III read his own version to the Lords in Council, but Pitt saw that his was entered in the journals of the Lower House, printed for the nation and circulated in the colonies.

Sir James Hodges, the town clerk, who superintended the drafting of petitions and addresses, had a genuine respect for the Great Commoner. He usually sent Pitt notices of addresses to the throne, and took care that reference should be made to the assiduity and integrity of the King's Councillors. But the town clerk was not a man who could entirely forget his own interests in attachment to those of a leader. His

---

[1] Chat. MSS. 53, Wal. Pringle to Pitt, S. Christopher's, Feb. 27, 1760.
[2] Pitt's speech on the address to the King, Nov. 13, 1755. Thackeray, vol. i., p. 227.

postscript to the letter in which he congratulated Pitt
on the capture of Louisburg is characteristic.

"P.S.—If knighthood be offered, I shall have no
objection to be one of your making. If it will be
agreeable to you, it will be much so to my friends, but
it must be offered in such manner as that it may not
be supposed I have before thought of it."[1]

As the first year of the new monarch's reign wore on
it became clear to the citizens of London that they
must choose between the royal and the ministerial
policy. Sir James sent Pitt early notice that the King
was to be congratulated on the conquest of Belleisle,[2]
and the address, which was presented on June 16,
plainly supported Pitt's vigorous measures and depre-
cated the peaceful designs of the Patriot King and his
favourites. After the usual formalities came one of
those perorations which Pitt described as " big with a
million in every line." [3]

"On our part, permit us humbly to assure your
Majesty, that your faithful citizens of London will
with an unwearied zeal and cheerfulness contribute
to support a vigorous prosecution of this just and
necessary war ; until your Majesty, having sufficiently
vindicated the honour of your crown and secured the
trade, navigation and possessions of your subjects,
shall enjoy the blessing and the glory of giving repose
to Europe, of wholly attending to and promoting
the virtue and happiness of your people and cultivating all the softer arts of peace."

But George III cared little for money which was to
be spent on war, or indeed on anything except the
softer arts of peace, which his disloyal subjects stigmatised as political bribery and corruption. On
October 2, Pitt resigned on the question of declaring

---

[1] Chat. MSS. 40, James Hodges to Pitt, Guildhall, Aug. 23, 1758.
[2] Chat. MSS. 40.
[3] Grenville Papers, Pitt to Grenville, Oct. 18, 1760.

war upon Spain. When the news first reached the city there was great indignation, and it was proposed to petition the King as to why Mr. Pitt had been dismissed. Then came the astounding news that the Great Commoner, the leader of the independent members, had accepted a pension from the King and a title for his wife. The outcry of " pensioner " and " Lady Cheat'em " that disgraced the city was a testimony to the reputation Pitt had hitherto enjoyed. Another statesman might have accepted such favours without remark ; but the Great Commoner had been thought above suspicion.

The cloud was dispersed by a letter which Pitt sent to the town clerk, explaining his reasons for resigning the seals and accepting a pension. The city returned to their allegiance, and presented the fallen leader with an address in which they declared that :

" The City of London, as long as they have any memory, cannot forget that you accepted the seals when this nation was in the most deplorable circumstances to which any country can be reduced, our trade exposed to the enemy, our credit, as if we expected to become bankrupts, sunk to the lowest pitch ; that there was nothing to be found but despondency at home and contempt abroad. The city must also for ever remember that when you resigned the seals, our armies and navies were victorious, our trade secure and flourishing more than in peace, our public credit restored, and people readier to lend than ministers to borrow ! " [1]

Pitt's visit to the city on Lord Mayor's day, when his magnificent reception at the Guildhall far exceeded the welcome given to the royal guests, has often been criticised severely.[2] The implied slight to the King was in the worst possible taste, and Pitt is said to have

---

[1] " Thackeray," vol. i., p. 595.
[2] Horace Walpole, " George III." *Cf.* B. Williams, " Pitt," vol. ii., p. 121.

much regretted the incident. Yet he was but following his usual custom of honouring the corporation with his presence on that anniversary.[1] The court party were the real aggressors. George III and Bute had formed a plan to capture the city,[2] and though Newcastle took every precaution that " Mr. Pitt should not hear of it," the plot became known to Beckford, and he insisted that his friend and patron should put the city to the test.

During the weary years of opposition and retirement that followed, Pitt's connection was necessarily more with individual citizens than with the city as a body ; although he always passionately supported the latter when its rights and liberties were threatened. The city's hopes were high when his second ministry was formed. Once more the people of England had given a minister to their King. The repeal of the Stamp Act was brought about by the clamour of the merchants, who saw their trade threatened ; and once more Pitt voiced their grievances. On the day of the repeal the Lobby of the House, the Court of Requests, and the avenues were blocked by American merchants. When the Great Commoner appeared the whole crowd pulled off their hats and cheered, some enthusiasts following his chair home with shouts and benedictions.[3]

The city grieved when Pitt accepted a peerage ; but when it became clear that his health and power were gone, individual citizens remained faithful in their attachment to the great leader. Many and various were the offerings which the Earl of Chatham was humbly requested to accept—old prints, pamphlets, rare books, numerous remedies for his gout, and above all provisions, " a barrel of mead," " a basket of game," " a haunch of venison," " smoaked tongues,

---

[1] Chat. MSS. 40, Hodges to Pitt, Oct. 30, 1759.
[2] Addit. MSS. 35425, ff. 250, 252 ; 32930, ff. 132, 222, 321.
[3] Horace Walpole, " George III," vol. ii., p. 212.

pine cones and cabbage seed from that very Northern climate of Archangel."[1]   It would seem that the good merchants had heard of the sick man's capricious appetite, and the succession of chickens that were always roasting and boiling in his kitchen.   For all these seasonable gifts Pitt invariably returned courteous thanks.

"The royal venison, which is extremely fine, will have a better flavour by coming through the city to Hayes from the friendly hand of Mr. Sheriff Sayre."[2]

But what Chatham prized most was the accurate information on American affairs that many of his city friends were able to procure for him.   Sheriff Sayre himself was one channel of information.   In the autumn of 1774 he sent Chatham letters from "a very eminent merchant of New York," and noted that he said "nothing of overstepping the laws of trade and breaking through the principles upon which our union ought to be established."[3]   Other of Chatham's informants took a more gloomy view of the case.   William Lee, another city sheriff, writing about the same time, said, that though it was clear to him that in general America was perfectly willing and desirous of remaining subject to a parliamentary control of her commerce, yet he feared that "the intemperate folly of an ill-advised ministry would urge the Americans to demands that they would not otherwise have thought of for a century to come."[4]

In reply to these letters Chatham declared "nothing can be so interesting in the present critical moment as authentic information relating to America.   I therefore esteem it a particular favour to receive such communications from you in any way most convenient to yourself."[5]

---

[1] Various letters in Chatham MSS.
[2] "Almon," vol. ii., p. 382, Chatham to Sayre, Hayes, Aug. 28, 1774.
[3] Chat. MSS. 55, Stephen Sayre to Chatham, Nov. 16, 1774.
[4] Chat. MSS. 48, Lee to Pitt, Sept. 25, 1774.
[5] "Almon," vol. ii., p. 379.

After Chatham had laid his plan for conciliating the differences between Great Britain and her American colonies before the House of Lords, the corporation of the city of London voted him their thanks for so humane a measure.

Chatham thanked " the Lord Mayor, Aldermen and Commons in Common Council assembled for the signal honour they had been pleased to confer on the mere discharge of his duty in a moment of impending calamity." [1]

Three months later, when the expected blow fell, Stephen Sayre sent Chatham the dreaded news post-haste :

" My Lord,
    " The Horrid Tragedy is commenced, there has been a battle near Concord." [2]

The year before the outbreak of hostilities the death of Thomas Hollis had deprived Chatham of the advice of one of the few men with whom he was ever upon at all intimate terms.

Thomas Hollis has been described by a contemporary as " a gentleman possessed of a large fortune, above the half of which he devotes to charities." [3]   He was the son and grandson of a merchant, and in his youth he received some commercial training ; but his wealth enabled him to devote his time to more congenial pursuits.   He was an ardent politician, but finding he could not enter parliament without favour or bribery, he decided to propagate his republican theories by means of literature ; and became a staunch supporter of the learned societies of London and other cities.   He sincerely admired the Great Commoner, and a mutual admiration for Oliver Cromwell and Milton was a bond of union between two very

---

1 " Almon," vol. ii., p. 379.
2 Chat. MSS. 55, Stephen Sayre to Chatham, London, May 29, 1775.
3 Chat. Corr. 2, p. 200.

dissimilar characters. Mr. Hollis spent his later years
at an old farm-house in Dorset, and when the Pitt
family were established at Burton Pynsent, visits
were exchanged. Chatham's children were an un-
failing source of wonder and delight to the kindly
philosopher. He walked in the fields with them, and
answered young William's precocious questions most
patiently.[1] A letter he wrote to Lord and Lady
Chatham after a visit at Burton Pynsent, which had
been extended in order that he might be present at
the performance of a play which the children were
rehearsing, is quaintly characteristic of the man and
his relations with the Pitt family.

"Thomas Hollis has the honor to present his best
compliments and thanks to Lord and Lady Chatham
for their very kind reception of him at Burton Pynsent,
and for the very singular and truly elegant entertainment of which they were pleased to make him par-
taker. An entertainment that he never thinks of
but with applause and wonder! Plutarch himself,
that refined good man, had he seen it must have been
delighted, and given equal rank at once to the Family
of Chatham with the Gracchi!

"He takes the liberty to send Lord Chatham an
abstract from Mr. Boyle's Philosophical works, relating to the prevention of the rot in sheep; and three
publications from Boston in New England, which
tend to show a people of strong sense and virtue in
the rough upon the rise.

"He requests the favour of Lady Chatham to
accept a basket of game. And he begs his most particular respects and acknowledgement to Lord Pitt,
Lady Hester, Lady Hariat and the two younger
Gentlemen. It is hard to guess, in what way this as-
tonishing young set would show themselves in Comedy
did they take to it."[2]

---

[1] Chat. Corr., vol. iv., p. 269.
[2] Chat. MSS. 40, Hollis to Chatham, Nov. 28, 1772.

As Hollis was in constant communication with American merchants,[1] his information was much valued by Chatham and ungrudgingly given by the loyal adherent, who boasted that " Many people have admired Lord Chatham easily throughout his vast public orations, and but few considered have known him in the purity, elegance, splendour and happiness of his own private domesticity." [2]

It is significant that while Lord Shelburne was never received by his colleague except by appointment in a drawing-room, formally dressed with stick and hat and without book or paper,[3] Thomas Hollis was allowed to romp with the Great Commoner's children and exchange ideas with their father on philosophical and political subjects.

Many of his contemporaries scoffed at the eulogies which Chatham pronounced upon the city fathers.[4] That his connection with the city was advantageous to himself is beyond question, but it is equally certain that the Great Commoner had a genuine respect for the civic dignitaries. The city was a little republic too wealthy to be bought, too self-interested and intelligent to follow any but an efficient leader. There is a note of sincerity in the speech in which Chatham defended the city in the House of Lords.

" When I mentioned the Livery of London I thought I saw a sneer upon some faces ; but let me tell you, My Lords, that although I have the honour to sit in this House, as a Peer of the realm, I am proud, coinciding as I do with these honest citizens in opinion, of the honour of associating my name with theirs." [5]

Two years later, when the Lord Mayor and Aldermen and Commons of the City of London petitioned

---

[1] Letters of Andrew Elliot to Thomas Hollis, Mass. Hist. Soc., series iv., vol. iv.
[2] Chat. MSS. 40.
[3] Fitzmaurice, " Life of Shelburne."
[4] Mrs. Montague's Corr., vol. iv., p. 79.
[5] " Thackeray," vol. ii., p. 193. Chatham on the City Petition, 1776.

that St. Paul's might be the last resting-place of the
Earl of Chatham, they reminded the King that that
illustrious statesman had " condescended to become
our fellow-citizen." And when the desire of the city
had to give way before the nation's claim the citizens
of London placed a fitting monument in their Guildhall to William Pitt, who raised his nation " to an high
pitch of prosperity and glory " . . . " by commerce
for the first time united with and made to flourish by
war."

CHAPTER III

PITT'S AFRICAN POLICY

Trade the chief motive of Pitt's African policy.—The English position in Africa in 1756.—Cumming's advice to Pitt.—The expeditions of 1758 against Senegal and Goree.—The value of the conquests tested by trade values.—Pitt's reasons for objecting to the cession of Goree.

PITT's African policy has been almost universally neglected by modern historians;[1] yet it formed an integral part of his general plan for an empire of trade, and, in many respects, was a most characteristic piece of his statecraft. The sole object of the expeditions which he sent against Senegal and Goree was to make war for and upon trade. The plan had been suggested to Pitt by a merchant, and merchant adventurers helped to carry it through. On this occasion he readily accepted advice from an unofficial quarter, and made a skilful use of his informant's peculiar knowledge; nor did he spare any pains on his own account in carrying out the plan which he had borrowed from another.[2] Probably, when Pitt took office in 1756, he knew as little about the West Coast of Africa as most men of his day. The climate was so deadly and the voyage so dangerous that there were few visitors to the Gambia or the Gold Coast except adventurous

---

[1] Basil Williams, in his " Life of Pitt," gives a narrative of the expeditions against Goree and Senegal, but does not devote any space to a detailed study of the policy which directed them. W. Frewin Lord gives the best account of the expeditions in his " Lost Possessions of England."

[2] *Cf.* Pitt's directions for the expeditions. P.R.O. State Papers, Domestic Entry Books, 229, 230, and 231. Also C.O. 267, 12. Pitt dictated these letters, which gout prevented him from signing, at a time when his doctor said continuance in office would kill him.

traders; and it was usually to their interest to keep their discoveries to themselves. While Secretary of State, Pitt gained his knowledge of African affairs from private traders, the African Company, and the Board of Trade. The records of the two last, supplemented by the Chatham Papers, give a vivid picture of the English position in Africa about the middle of the eighteenth century.

In 1756 no European power possessed any part of West Africa, but there were English, French, Dutch, Portuguese, and Danish factories on the coast; trading stations for which their occupiers paid an annual quit-rent to the native chiefs. These stations, like those in India, served the double purpose of warehouses and forts. The French factories were under the control of their East India Company, who enjoyed a monopoly of the French trade on the coast. The English forts were maintained by the committee of the Company of Merchants Trading to Africa, who received an annual grant from the government for the purpose. Membership of this Company was open to any British subject on the payment of a forty-shilling entrance fee.[1] The African trade consisted principally of slaves, gum, gold-dust, and ivory. The English commerce was confined to two districts, the Gambia and the Gold Coast. There were ten English factories on the Gold Coast in various stages of decay,[2] better calculated to awe the natives than to withstand the attack of a civilised enemy. Their trade was almost entirely confined to slaves, the natives of the neighbouring districts being of splendid physique, though of a correspondingly ferocious disposition.[3]

---

[1] Cf. W. Cunningham, "History of Industry and Commerce, Modern Times," part i., p. 26. C. M. H., vol. vii., chap. 6, by Benians, p. 187. "The Records of the English African Companies by C. H. Jenkinson," Trans. of Royal Hist. Soc., series iii., vol. vii.

[2] C.O. 267, 11, Engineers' Report, 1757.

[3] Alfred Ellis, "History of the Gold Coast." Cf. Walton Claridge, "History of the Gold Coast," vol. i., p. 152.

James Fort, the only English factory in Senegambia, was situated on James Island, at the mouth of the easily navigable Gambia. The whole of James Island was fortified, and its arrangement was very similar to that of the other European communities in West Africa. Inside the outer walls there were two slave houses, one for the men and the other for the women, to the latter of which a kitchen was attached. Each house had an exercising ground. Near by was the Governor's kitchen and storehouse ; next came the storehouses for the trade goods, then the artificer's quarters and the barracks for the Company's soldiers. There were huts for the slaves belonging to the fort, a granary, a lime-kiln, a saw-pit, a smith's shop, guns for defence and small guns used for firing salutes. The fort itself was in the centre of the island. It was a square building with four bastions, and contained the Governor's room, the Council room, the magazine, and the cistern, besides apartments for the Governor's staff. The trade consisted chiefly in slaves.

There was constant friction between James Fort and the French stations at Albreda, on the Gambia, and at Fort Louis, and the island of Goree which commanded the Senegal trade. As in India, the French and English traders stirred up the natives against one another ; privateering was rife, and piracy not unknown. The Moors and Negroes occasionally copied the Europeans, made prizes of distressed ships and held their crews for ransom.[1] Fever, revolts among the slaves, and murder among the whites were common ills.[2] The Governors of the forts and their assistants were usually men who, as they themselves declared, had risked their lives and abandoned their poor families for a little pelf ;[3] who thought more about private trade than public service. Their salaries were

---

[1] C.O. 267, 12, Newton to Pitt, Jan. 1, 1760.
[2] C.O. 388, 47, and African Co., 30, f. 170.
[3] African Co., 30, f. 107.

inadequate, and their spasmodic attempt to put the
forts under their care in a proper state of defence
were hampered by lack of skilled workmen. Brick-
layers, masons, and carpenters could not be persuaded
to try the climate of Senegambia.[1] On one occasion
the secretary of the committee wrote joyfully to the
Governor of James Fort that he had secured a mason
at last; but the good man thought better of his
venture when he saw the ships at Gravesend, and ran
away.[2] For over two years a solitary white bricklayer
laboured at the fortifications of James Fort. Although
not highly skilled, he was a willing workman, and a
person of great importance to the little settlement.
In 1756 the Governor writes joyfully, " Broomhill,
our only bricklayer, holds out to a miracle,"[3] but
two years later sadly records the " mortifying
circumstance " that the wise fellow had left at the
expiration of his time.[4] Urgent requests were sent
home for a good smith, " the old smith Kenny being
quite wore out by old age ; "[5] and bitter complaints
were made of Hughes, the carpenter, whom the sur-
veyor declared was the worst he ever saw, and unable
to learn to do anything.[6] One tradesman is described
as " a very drunken, insolent fellow, and will not work
but when he pleases."[7] The Governor was provoked,
but feared he was too valuable a personage to be
treated with other than moral suasion, and wrote home
to the committee for instructions on this point. The
problem solved itself ; drunkards did not live long at
James Fort. Young slaves were bought and trained
for the castle work, but found very unsatisfactory. It
is noteworthy that the slave-traders themselves

---

[1] African Co., 29, ff. 78 and 84.
[2] Ibid., f. 80.
[3] Ibid., 30, f. 160.
[4] Ibid., f. 220, April 23, 1758.
[5] Ibid., f. 127, Jan. 10, 1756.
[6] Ibid., f. 113.
[7] Ibid., f. 112.

calculated that one free labourer was worth four slaves.[1]

Nor was it easy for the Company to procure good soldiers to man their forts. In the eighteenth century there was better service for English adventurers than a rat-trap existence on the pestilential African coast. Often the only men the Company could obtain were old decrepit creatures who required nurses.[2]

Directly war was declared with France the African Company, knowing the weakness of James Fort, petitioned the Admiralty that a man-of-war might be stationed at Gambia.[3] At first their request was not favourably received, but help came from an unexpected quarter, and by the end of 1756 the most powerful man in England was hard at work planning for the safety of our African trade.

Soon after he became Secretary of State, Pitt received advances from Thomas Cumming, a Quaker merchant, who had a most suspiciously strange tale to tell.[4] Cumming declared that in 1749 he had chanced one day to be in London near the Royal Exchange, when he noticed four or five men in Eastern dress whom he thought were Turks. He spoke to them, and one of their number, who spoke English, told him that they were Moors, natives of that part of South Barbary called the Gum Coast. They and some of their countrymen had been seized by Dutch traders and carried to one of the Cape de Verde Islands as slaves. But the people of the island had refused to buy them, and the Dutchmen had left them on the island to shift for themselves, and sailed away with their companions, of whose fate they were ignorant. Soon after the departure of the Dutch

---

[1] C.O. 267, 12, Col. Newton to Pitt, Feb. 10, 1759.
[2] African Co., 30, f. 255.
[3] *Ibid.*, 29, f. 83, Secretary of Company to Governor of James Fort, May 27, 1756.
[4] C.O. 267, 12.

ship, an English vessel, bound for London, touched at the island, and the captain persuaded the Moors to go with him, promising to take them back to their own country on his return voyage. Cumming showed the strangers considerable kindness, and in return received a warm invitation to visit them in their own land.

About four months after this, Cumming returned to his home in New York, and shortly afterwards a shipowner of the city who was a great friend of his received a ship home from the Cape de Verde Islands, whose captain had kindly given a passage to the Moors' companions whom the Dutch traders had left at another of the islands. Cumming made the most of the chance which had again thrown these useful people in his way, " bestowing on them every favour and civility in his power," and obtaining another warm invitation to trade on the Gum Coast.

Five years later he was able to carry out a long-cherished plan. He sailed from London, where he now made his home, arrived safely at the Gum Coast, and met all his old friends. They made him welcome, and introduced him to their chief Amir, Sultan, King of the Legibbilli, who gave him a charter granting him a right to trade in the country of the Legibbilli. The enterprising merchant seized his opportunity, and during the next two years sent several ships to trade with the Moors. This trade consisted in the barter of European manufactures for gum, which the Moors brought to the Barbary coast from a considerable distance.

The French East India Company treated the few English traders who found their way to the Gum Coast as interlopers, and tried to prevent the natives from trading with them. But the Moors, who knew that competition raised prices, and also found it more convenient to sell to the English ships on the coast than to have to carry the gum down to the French depôts at Desart and Padore, were very willing to open their trade to British subjects.[1]   Indeed, in 1756, the French East India Company was in such difficulties that their African trade was greatly neglected.   For lack of commodities to barter, French traders had to ask credit of the Moorish merchants, who naturally raised their prices and sought other customers.[2] Cumming's good friend, the King of the Legibbilli, even succeeded in wringing permission from the Governor of Fort Louis for the English interlopers to trade freely.[3]

While paying his visit to the Gum Coast in 1754, Cumming was much struck by the bad relations that existed between the Moors and the French.   King Amir made him a formal offer to help the King of England to capture Senegal and Goree.   The good Quaker's only motive in going to the Gum Coast had been to make his fortune, but he at once saw the national importance of Amir's suggestion, and promised him he would deliver his message to King George III, should he go to war with the King of France.

Directly war was declared, Cumming called upon the Secretary of State and explained the advantages to be gained by an attack upon Senegal and Goree. Fox sent him to the Earl of Halifax and Lord Anson ; the latter, who knew the Gum Coast well, approved the plan.   After the resignation of Fox and Anson, Cumming applied to the Duke of Cumberland, who " heard him with princely attention, as became a prince of the blood and the son of a king," but did nothing.

Finally, the industrious merchant appealed to Temple, Boscawen, and Pitt, who immediately gave the plan their warmest support.[4]   Pitt drafted a

---

[1] C.O. 389, 30, f. 521.
[2] C.O. 267, 12 (Intercepted French Letters).
[3] C.O. 389, 30, f. 517.
[4] Chat. MSS. 30, Cumming to Pitt, Jan. 28 and Feb. 1, 1757 ; Chat. Corr. 4221, Pitt to Cumming, Feb. 9, 1757.

magnificent letter " to the High and Glorious Monarch, the Mighty and Right Noble Prince, Amir Sultan, King of Legibbilli, from his most affectionate friend George R." Amir was directed to give entire credence to the bearer, Thomas Cumming, and to the commander of the King's great ships of war whom he would introduce to him, and invited to assist them in an attack upon the French forts.[1] The expedition was almost ready to sail in March,[2] but the plan was abandoned after Pitt's resignation in April. Two men-of-war were sent to Gambia, and arrived safely in August.[3] Yet the position of James Fort was considered so desperate that in November it was rumoured in London that it had been captured by the enemy. French privateers from Goree captured several English trading vessels at the mouth of the Gambia, but no attack was made on the fort.[4]

Soon after Pitt was restored to office he again turned his attention to African affairs. On January 12 he sent detailed instructions for the preparation of ships and arms to the Lords of the Admiralty and the Master-General of the Ordnance.[5] The expedition sailed from Plymouth on March 9. It consisted of His Majesty's ship the *Nassau* of sixty-four guns, the *Harwich* of fifty guns, the *Rye* of twenty-four guns, with the *Swan* sloop and two busses. Captain Marsh was in command of the expedition, Major Mason had charge of 200 marines, and Captain Walker of the artillery.[6] Mr. Cumming accompanied the

---

[1] C.O. 267, 12, f. 1, Feb. 1, 1757.

[2] S. P. Dom., Entry Books 229, f. 134, Pitt to the Lords of the Admiralty, March 1, 1757. C.O. 267, 12, Pitt to the Duke of Marlborough, March 1, 1757. Chat. MSS. 30, Cumming to Pitt, Feb. 1, 1757.

[3] African Co., 30, f. 201. The Governor of James Fort to the African Co., Aug. 23, 1757.

[4] *Ibid.*, June 25, and Oct. 23, 1757.

[5] C.O. 267, 12.

[6] Addit. MSS. Brit. Mus. 32880, f. 393. Extract of Account received from the Coast of Africa, June 10, 1758, by Capt. Wilson of the *Swan* sloop.

expedition, whose success was largely due to his knowledge of the river Senegal.[1]

On June 24 the expedition arrived at the mouth of the river, and prepared to attack Fort Louis, as Cumming well knew the bar of the river was very dangerous on account of the shifting of the sand and the roughness of the surf.[2] The entrance was carefully sounded, and on June 29 the *Swan* sloop and the boats succeeded in getting over the bar. Seven French vessels made some show of attacking, but were repulsed and driven up the river. Fort Louis was then at the mercy of the English, for the French had trusted entirely to the difficulty of the bar of the river, and the fort was a crazy building of more pretensions than strength. It boasted half bastions, a banquette and parapette, but was built of clay and soft brick plastered over. The magazine and barracks were under the parapette, which made it dangerous to fire anything above a three-pounder.[3] The English marines and seamen got the artillery ashore and dragged them up to the fort.[4] But when they prepared to attack, deputies arrived from the superior council of Senegal with articles of capitulation. On May 2 Major Mason and the marines took possession of the fort.[5]

It was a rich haul, for besides 230 prisoners and ninety-two pieces of cannon, there were 500 slaves, 400 tons of gum, a considerable quantity of gold dust, between 40,000 and 50,000 dollars, and a year's supply of goods for barter, besides stores and provisions. Two men-of-war were despatched from Senegal to make an attack upon Goree, but were repulsed with considerable loss. They went to James Fort for water,

---

[1] Chatham Papers, 30.   C.O. 389, 30, f. 509.
[2] C.O. 389, 30, f. 509.
[3] Chat. MSS. 100. Copy of a letter from Capt. John Forbes to Duncan, Fort Louis, Aug. 20, 1758.
[4] C.O. 267, 12, Major Mason to Cleveland, May 3, 1758.
[5] *Ibid.*, Captain Walker to Cleveland, May 3, 1758.

and then made an attack upon Albreda, but without success.[1]

The news of the capture of Senegal was received with joy in England on June 10.[2] Lord Anson declared that the conquest was of more consequence than was generally imagined, predicted that the French would " sit down very uneasy with the loss of it," and urged that measures should be taken immediately to secure Fort Louis.[3] This was Pitt's first care. He received the official detailed account of the capture of Senegal on June 13, and wrote the same day to the Lords of the Admiralty and Secretary at War, directing that ships and men who had been collected for a voyage to Jamaica should be despatched at once to Senegal.[4] An engineer was sent at once to strengthen Fort Louis,[5] and Pitt wrote to Major Mason appointing him Governor of the Fort, and instructing him to " carefully endeavour to discover the nature of the trade carried on up the said river Senegal, and also the various productions and sources of the riches of those countries," and to give all the assistance and protection in his power to any British traders who might come to Fort Louis.[6] Mason appears to have carried out his instructions carefully, though he had considerable difficulty with the natives. He deserves credit for the prompt way in which he relieved the French forts at Padore and Galam, trading stations up the river which had been included in the capitulation, though the settlement at the latter place had to be abandoned afterwards, as the district was peculiarly deadly to Europeans.[7]

[1] African Co., 30, f. 247. James Fort, July 18, 1758. Tobias Lisle and Council to the Committee.
[2] Addit. MSS. 32, 880.
[3] Addit. MSS. 32881, f. 111, Anson to Newcastle, *Royal George* at sea, June 29, 1758.
[4] C.O. 267, 12.
[5] S. P. Dom., Entry Books, 230, f. 13.
[6] C.O. 267, 12, Pitt to Mason, May 13 and 15, 1758.
[7] C.O. 267, 12, and African Co., 30.

Meanwhile Pitt was busily employed in fitting out another expedition to attack Goree[1]. Captain the Hon. Augustus Keppel was given the command on October 6, and urged to set out without delay, as Pitt had information that the enemy were preparing to reinforce Goree. Keppel was detained at Portsmouth and again at Cork, where he picked up some of his transports. When he wrote to Pitt to explain his delay, he received a peremptory reply, urging haste at any sacrifice.[2] In November the Expeditionary Force sailed from Cork, and on December 14 anchored in the Santa Cruz roads off Teneriffe, where a rendezvous for the straggling squadron had been arranged. Here Keppel lost two of his ships in a violent storm.[3] On the evening of December 28 the squadron arrived off Goree. The next morning the ships made an attack on the forts and batteries of the island. The Governor soon sent a flag of truce, offering to capitulate if allowed the honours of war. The terms were refused, and a fresh attack begun ; but shortly afterwards the garrison surrendered at discretion. Two days later, Lieutenant-Colonel Worge and the troops under his command took possession of the fort.

Afterwards a dispute took place between the sailors, who claimed all the credit as well as the booty, and the soldiers, who complained that : " The French not doing their duty prevented us from what we would have attempted for the sake of our country." The case was submitted to Pitt, who decided in favour of the soldiers. On January 12, 1759, Keppel left Colonel Newton in charge of the garrison at Goree, and sailed for Senegal with all his squadron, except one frigate which he left to protect the Goree trade. Four days later he

---

[1] S. P. Dom., Entry Books, 30, Pitt to the Lords of the Admiralty, Sept. 5, 6, and 30 ; to the Master-General of the Ordnance, Sept. 1 and 9, and Oct. 4, 1758 ; and to the Secretary of War, Sept. 6, Oct. 2, 1758.   See Appendix.
[2] C.O. 267, 12, Pitt to Keppel, Oct. 16, 1758.
[3] *Ibid.*, Keppel to Pitt, Dec. 19, 1758.

arrived at Fort Louis, where, according to Pitt's
instructions, he left Colonel Worge, who superseded
Captain Mason as Governor of the station. On
March 1 Keppel arrived at Spithead, and sent Pitt a
full account of the expedition.[1] During the next two
months Pitt received further information from Worge
and Newton ; he immediately attended to every
detail of their requests, sending them presents for the
natives and special stores.[2] Worge was also directed
to give all the assistance in his power to the officers
of the African Company, who would be sent to the
Senegal to enquire into the gum trade.[3]

On April 10 Pitt instructed the Board of Trade to
enquire into and report upon the commercial advantages that might accrue to the nation from the acquisition of Senegal. At Pitt's directions the Board collected evidence from Cumming, Major Mason, and
others well informed on African matters. On June 1
the report was presented to the King.[4] This report
gives a very detailed account of African trade, and its
accuracy can be tested by the information sent to Pitt
by Mason, Worge, and Newton. These agree in all
essentials, though there is an interesting difference
of opinion as to how the trade might be best secured
to Great Britain. All agreed that the chief advantage
of the conquest lay in the command of the gum trade.
The annual amount of the gum trade of the whole
river was estimated at between 4,000 and 8,000 tons.
As previously mentioned, it was brought by the Moors
from the interior twice a year, after the half-yearly
gathering in December and March.[5] There were
two places of barter—one called the Desart, about
fifteen leagues higher up the river than Fort Louis ;

---

[1] C.O. 267, 12, Keppel to Pitt. Torbay at Spithead, March 1, 1759.
[2] *Ibid.*, see Appendix.
[3] *Ibid.*, March 15, 1759, Pitt to Worge.
[4] C.O. 389, 30, ff. 507-535.
[5] Entick, " History of the Late War," vol. iii., p. 67.

the other, which was known as the Cock, was five leagues
beyond the Desart. The French had had no settlement at either of these places. When they received
notice of the arrival of the Moors, they sent buyers
to purchase the gum and small vessels to bring it down
to the fort.

The gum trade differed a good deal from the slave
traffic. The Moors were educated men. Their kings
wrote in fine Arabic, and attached their seals to official
documents. Some of them were also Marmouds,
and forbidden by their religion to touch strong drink.
In place of the brandy, iron bars and beads, which formed
the staple medium of exchange in the slave trade, the
Moors demanded blue Manchester goods, coarse brown
sugar, sealing-wax, large size writing-paper, arms, powder
and ball.[1] Eighteenth-century economists hoped that
the gum trade might become a close national monopoly:
a means not only of encouraging English manufactures,
but also of ruining those of France.[2] Gum senega
was largely used in the manufacture of French silk
and linen. Would not the price of these commodities
be raised if the French had to give a high price for
English gum ?

Next in value came the slave trade. This was
carried on all the year round at Senegal and Goree,
and estimated at 1,200 slaves a year. Small quantities
of ivory and gold were also exported from Senegambia.
A considerable quantity of cotton was grown round
Senegal, and some of the inhabitants of Fort Louis
were disposed to teach the negroes to spin and weave
it in the English manner. But Governor Worge
put an end to the enterprise, and wrote to Pitt in
righteous indignation. "I have put a stop to them,
and as I found them in ignorance so I shall keep them,
as it would be detrimental to our manufactures." [3]

---

[1] C.O. 267, 12, Worge to Pitt, Senegal, March 24, 1759.
[2] C.O. 389, 30.
[3] C.O. 267, 12, Worge to Pitt, Senegal, March 24, 1759.

In curious contrast is the encouragement given by Pitt and Governor Worge to adventurers who offered to explore up the Senegal into the interior.[1] It was felt that Africa was a land of vast possibilities, but the imperial ideal of the eighteenth century was exploitation rather than development.

In August Pitt received information that the French were likely to attempt the recapture of Senegal and Goree. He at once ordered a reinforcement of 200 men for each.[2] The troops reached their destination in October.[3] In 1760 and 1761 the British trade to Senegambia flourished exceedingly.[4] After Pitt's resignation and the declaration of war with Spain, grave fears were entertained by the African Committee for the safety of Senegal and Goree.[5] They were still more alarmed when they heard that it was proposed to restore Goree to France at the peace. They petitioned against such a dangerous cession, but were told that their objections came too late. For, as a contemporary divine remarked, " the negociators were determined to have peace at any price, and drove on, Jehu-like, regarding neither the glory of the crown nor the voice of the nation." [6]

Pitt consistently opposed the restoration of Goree. The very name of the island was a corruption of the Dutch word Goerée, a harbour. It had always been a first-class privateering station, an African Dunkirk. Its trade was not considerable, but its retention or demolition was essential to the safety of Senegal. In the earlier negotiations which Pitt had conducted he had refused to surrender either Senegal or Goree, and the French had agreed to accept some third place

---

[1] C.O. 267, 12, Worge to Pitt, Senegal, Jan. 14, 1760, and July 11, 1760.

[2] *Ibid.*, Pitt to Governor Worge, the Lords of the Admiralty, and the Secretary of War, Aug. 9, 1759.

[3] *Ibid.*, Worge to Pitt, Oct. 19, 1759.

[4] *Ibid.*, July 4, 1760, and May 19, 1761.

[5] African Co., 30, ff. 455 and 462.

[6] Entick, " History of the Late War," vol. v., p. 436.

on the African coast. Pitt was therefore justified in pronouncing the cession not only unsafe but unnecessary.[1]

Goree was restored to France on June 10, 1763, after having been put in good repair,[2] and in a few years again became a flourishing privateering station, and a perpetual source of annoyance to English traders at Senegal.[3] Fort Louis was handed over to the African Company, who received an annual grant of £7,000 from the Government for its maintenance.[4] Cumming petitioned the Board of Trade to grant a monopoly of the gum trade north of Senegal to himself and the adventurous merchants who had so materially helped towards the capture of Fort Louis. But the eighteenth-century economists abhorred private monopolies as much as they cherished national corners, and, although he eventually received a small pension, the poor Quaker lived to regret bitterly that he had ever forsaken " the secrets and sweets of a mercantile trade " for the chances of war.[5]

Judged by the standards of his age, Pitt's African policy was undoubtedly successful. It deprived the enemy of a valuable source of revenue during the war, and correspondingly increased the resources of Great Britain. It raised the price of negroes in the French West Indies to a prohibitive price, and weakened the French privateers which were partly manned by slaves.[6] There is nothing to show that the Great Commoner had enlightened ideas on the subject of slavery. His attention appears to have been first drawn to Africa by Cumming's stories of the gum trade. He was also interested in schemes for discovering gold

---

[1] Speech on the Preliminaries for Peace, 1762.
[2] C.O. 267, 12, Egremont to Worge, April 18, 1763.
[3] C.O. 389, 31, f. 253, Petition from the Board of Trade, Feb. 21, 1765.
[4] C.O. 267, 12.
[5] Chat. MSS. 30, and C.O. 389, 30 and 48, Petitions from Cumming.
[6] C.O. 389, 30, f. 479.

mines and exploring the interior. But although it was not his first consideration, Pitt by no means neglected the slave trade, and on one occasion promised to use his influence to get the traffic so regulated that the West Indies might have a continual supply of slaves at a cheap rate. It was left to his great son to discover the human element in this branch of African commerce.

CHAPTER IV

CANADA

" They seem to have lost sight of the great fundamental principle
that France is chiefly if not solely to be dreaded by us in the light of a
maritime and commercial power, and therefore by restoring to her all
the valuable West India Islands, and by our concessions in the Newfoundland fishery, we had given to her the means of recovering her
prodigious losses and of becoming once more formidable to us at sea."
—Pitt on the Preliminaries for Peace, 1762.

THE brilliant writer who has made the early history
of North America at once a classic and a romance,
has pointed out that when Pitt took office in 1756
the English conquest of Canada was no foregone
conclusion.[1] Some of the leading statesmen of the
day questioned not only whether it were possible, but
if it would be good policy, to drive the French entirely
from the continent.[2] Pitt had no such doubts ; ten
years before his first ministry he had come to the conclusion that the expulsion of the French was not only
possible, but absolutely necessary, for the safety of the
British colonists. Ten years of watchful observation
gave his opinion the force of a verdict.

Curiously enough, Pitt gained his first knowledge
of Canadian affairs from the Duke of Bedford, the
man who was to defeat Pitt's designs at the moment
of victory. As Paymaster of the Forces, he was
brought into communication with the Duke, who was
First Lord of the Admiralty from 1746 to 1748, and
then Secretary of State till 1750.[3] In 1746 Bedford

---

[1] Parkman, " Montcalm and Wolfe," vol. i., pp. 1-4.
[2] *Cf*. B. Williams, vol. i., p. 296.
[3] Woburn MSS. 48.

and Pitt were the only English ministers who seriously advocated an attack upon the commercial empire of France. When, in 1745, a handful of New England fishermen and farmers captured Louisburg, the American Dunkirk, Pitt and Bedford were thrilled,[1] and the former did all in his power to persuade the Duke of Newcastle to send an expedition against Quebec in 1746.[2] This bold plan originated with William Vaughan, of New Hampshire, a substantial merchant who owned a fishing station at Martinicus, and Shirley, the enterprising governor of Massachusetts. Shirley guaranteed that the colonies would raise provincial troops if Great Britain would send a squadron and eight battalions of regulars ; a junction of forces was to be effected at Louisburg, Quebec captured, and all Canada brought under the British flag.

Bedford and Pitt made a careful study of the facts submitted to them by Shirley, Vaughan, and Admiral Warren, who had commanded the squadron which assisted at the capture of Louisburg.[3] The memorial which Bedford sent to Newcastle is significant, as foreshadowing Pitt's Canadian policy. The First Lord of the Admiralty began his report by stating that the importance of the reduction of Canada, Louisiana, and in fact of the whole French Empire in America, was so self-evident that he would deal shortly with that matter, and confine himself to five propositions which he did not believe would be denied by anyone at all conversant in trade and with the state of the American colonies. " In the first place," the Duke continues, " this conquest will secure to us for ever the whole fish and fur trade, by both of which the French gain

---

[1] Bed. Corr., vol. i., p. 54, Bedford to Admiral Warren, Oct. 30, 1745, and Pitt to Bedford, Aug. 2, 1745.
[2] Addit. MSS.
[3] C.O. 42, 13, Bedford to Newcastle, March 24, 1746. Chatham Papers, 95. This bundle contains copies of various letters to and from the Duke of Newcastle on American affairs, also a copy of Vaughan's report on Newfoundland, Cape Breton, Nova Scotia, and Canada.

yearly such vast sums, besides the means of training up great numbers of seamen, and thereby gaining a prodigious additional strength to their naval force.

" Secondly, by this they will be debarred supplying sugar islands with provisions, lumber, and all things necessary for carrying on their sugar and indigo works, which must in the end prove their ruin, or at least enable our sugar planters to undersell them, which I fear is far from being the case at present.

" Thirdly, the trade of old France must inevitably be greatly diminished if the two foregoing propositions are just : as both the inhabitants of Canada (as well Indian as French), as also those of the sugar islands, take off vast quantities of French manufactures in return for the respective commodities of their own growth.

" Fourthly, France will no longer have it in her power to build ships of war in America, and will be obliged to furnish herself with great masts and other things absolutely necessary for the building of great ships from the Eastland county only ; which will be a great means of keeping her naval force within due bounds."[1]

Bedford's fifth proposition was that in the total expulsion of the French from North America lay the only security for the British colonies. Pitt acclaimed Bedford's views as " great and practicable," and assured the Duke that though he was alone in the ministry he had the support of the nation, and that with such a second all things were possible.[2]

The timidity of the Pelhams frustrated Bedford's designs. The embarkation of the forces he raised for the Quebec expedition was delayed till the temper and purse-strings of the provincials raised by Shirley were strained to their utmost limits ; whilst the Indians whom the Governor of New York had summoned to a

---

[1] C.O. 42, 13, Bedford to Newcastle, London, March 24, 1746.
[2] Bedford Corr., vol. i., p. 132, Pitt to Bedford, July 19, 1746.

council at Albany openly expressed their contempt when the plan was abandoned. As Paymaster of the Forces, it fell to Pitt to clear up the muddle, and secure compensation for nine American captains who had raised troops for the proposed expedition at their own expense.[1]

Pitt welcomed the truce of 1748, though it involved the restitution of Louisburg, because it brought peace, which he knew was urgently needed for the recuperation of the finances of Great Britain. He was anxious that his country should strengthen her sinews of war for the day when a new set of men and measures should warrant a trial of strength. For ten years he watched the progress of American affairs, fretted by his helplessness, insistent in his attempts to win a position of power in the Cabinet and a place in the confidence of his King. He watched the French refortify Louisburg, and knew that the British fishery was threatened ; he noted the linking up of the chain of forts from the St. Lawrence to the Mississippi, by which his rivals engrossed the Indian trade and hemmed in the British colonies. He saw French West Indian trade increase, and the British merchant everywhere undersold.[2]

What alarmed Pitt most of all was the position of affairs in Nova Scotia. France had ceded this ill-defined province to Great Britain by the treaty of Utrecht ; but the cession was almost nominal, as the Catholic Church kept the Acadians loyal to her eldest son, and they refused an oath of allegiance which might force them to take arms against him.[3] The obvious design of France to recover Nova Scotia was the spur that urged on the New Englanders to capture Louisburg. They believed that the fishery, their chief means of subsistence, was threatened, and regarded the

[1] C.O. 42, 13, Paymaster-General's Report, June 15, 1749.
[2] Chatham Papers, 95 and 98, and Speech of Dec. 9, 1762.
[3] Parkman, "Montcalm and Wolfe," vol. i., p. 90.

taking of the fort as a measure of defence rather than
of aggression.[1] At the treaty of Aix-la-Chapelle,
France confirmed the cession of " Acadia with her
ancient limits " to Great Britain, but afterwards
declared that the ancient limits included only the
Peninsula, and proceeded to build forts at Gaspereau
and Beauséjour, on the isthmus of Chignecto, and
establish another outpost on the River St. John, thus
controlling the land and sea routes from Quebec to
Cape Breton.[2]

Pitt at once saw the danger that threatened the
Newfoundland fisheries, which, he was assured by
memorialists, might become more valuable to England
than the mines of Mexico and Peru were to Spain.[3]
He tried to alarm Newcastle on this score, but without
success.[4] Four years later, when Braddock's ill-fated
expedition was sent to try to break the chain of forts
which was severing the British colonies from the
Indian trade, Pitt gave the ministry an early warning
that the force they were preparing was inadequate.[5]
His opinions were disregarded, Braddock and his men
were sacrificed.[6] French intrigues in Acadia were
allowed to flourish, till the uprooting of an innocent
population was the only means by which the land could
be cleared of strife. When Secretary of State, Pitt
made it his duty to enquire into the fate of those
Acadians who had been deported to the New England
colonies in 1755,[7] and to provide for the peopling
of the desolated land with Protestant labourers.[8]

As early as 1745 Chesterfield had warned Newcastle
that Pitt was to be feared for his talents and efficiency,

---

[1] Parkman, " Montcalm and Wolfe," Appendix.
[2] Bourinot, " Canada," p. 221.
[3] Chat. MSS. 98.
[4] Addit. MSS. 32721, Pitt to Newcastle, June 19, 1750.
[5] Addit. MSS. 35909.
[6] Bradley, " The Fight for North America."
[7] C.O. 5, 488, Pitt to the Lords of Trade, Nov. 7, 1757.
[8] Addit. MSS. 35913, f. 227.

and that if he were admitted to the ministry he would have the lead given him or take it.[1] By the beginning of 1758 Pitt had been given a share in the government, had taken the lead and made efficiency the keynote of British policy. There was nothing new in Pitt's scheme for the conquest of Canada except the skilful use he made of his own knowledge and the experience of others. In the eighteenth century few cared to brave the horrors of an Atlantic crossing in a sailing ship unless substantial compensation awaited on the other side. The evidence submitted by merchants to the Secretary of State was often biassed, but it was the best that could be obtained. Pitt made great use of the information supplied to him by the Society of London Merchants trading to Virginia and Maryland, and also employed captains of merchant ships whom they informed him had special knowledge of the American coast.[2]

Although no detail was too small for his attention, Pitt never lost sight of the great fundamental principle of his colonial policy, that France was " chiefly if not solely to be dreaded as a maritime and commercial power." He valued Canada for her fisheries and fur trade, which, like the African gum and slaves, were to have their allotted place in that great empire of trade which he designed should centre round the West Indies.[3] In 1758 Pitt's victories were decisive because they secured the command of all the French trade in North America. The capture of Louisburg secured the fishery and paved the way for the taking of Quebec, the citadel of Canadian commerce ; and when Forbes was successful in his expedition against Fort Du Quesne, which opened up the Western trade to the Southern colonies, the London merchants sent

---

[1] Addit. MSS. 32706, f. 221, Chesterfield to Newcastle, Feb. 17, 1745.
[2] Chatham Papers, 95.
[3] Speech on Preliminaries, 1762.

E

the Secretary of State a letter of hearty congratulation and thanks for the victory.[1] Pitt instructed the General to refortify the position ; he did, and gave the little wooden stockade he built the appropriate name of Pittsburg,[2] a name which now stands for a great commercial centre, a fitting memorial to the foresight of her founder.

But the real fight for Canada, as Pitt and the merchants trading to North America understood the phrase —that is, the fight for a monopoly of the Newfoundland fisheries—only began with the negociations for peace. Pitt had foreseen that it would be so; when Lord Hardwicke congratulated him on the taking of Quebec he replied, " Perhaps it is not too much to say that sustaining war, arduous as it has been and still is, may not be more difficult than properly and happily closing it.   The materials in His Majesty's hands are certainly very many and great ; and it is to be hoped that in working them up in the great edifice of a solid and general pacification of Europe there may be no confusion of languages, but that the workmen may understand one another." [3]

Pitt's forebodings were more than fulfilled ; he knew there were men who, even after Quebec had fallen, doubted the wisdom of expelling the French from Canada ; but in 1759 he could not have foreseen the speedy accession of George III which was to curtail his powers, or that the intervention of Spain would force his resignation.

Negociations for peace with France were opened on March 26, 1761, and for a time proceeded smoothly. Pitt demanded the complete cession of Canada, to which France perforce agreed. The struggle turned upon the fishery question. Pitt claimed for Great

---

[1] Chatham Papers, 96, London, Feb., 1759.
[2] Coll. Corr., vol. i., p. 409.
[3] Addit. MSS. 32897, f. 254, Pitt to Hardwicke, Hayes, Oct. 20, 1759.

Britain the exclusive right to fish in the Gulf of Newfoundland. To this term France retained an absolute refusal. A deadlock ensued. Pitt declared that if he signed a treaty without an exclusive right to the Newfoundland fishery he should be sorry he had recovered the use of his gouty right hand.[1] The Duc de Choiseul affirmed that if he gave up all the French fishing rights he would be stoned in the streets of Paris.[2] Pitt has often been blamed for his demand for a monopoly, but he was supported by many economists of his day. Mr Jenkinson (afterwards Lord Liverpool), an acknowledged authority on matters of trade,[3] declared that it was the opinion of all the great persons who had governed the colonies that Canada without the fisheries was hardly worth acceptance.[4] Henry McCulloch took the same view, and the instructions which the City of London gave to their representatives in 1761 show the value placed upon the fisheries by commercial men.

" That you entertain just sentiments of the importance of the conquests made this war by the British arms at the expense of much blood and treasure ; and that you will to the utmost of your power and abilities, oppose all attempts for giving up such places as may tend to lessen our present security, or by restoring the naval power of France render us subject to fresh hostilities from that hated enemy ; particularly that the sole and exclusive right of our acquisitions in North America and the fisheries be preserved to us." [5]

But before the autumn of 1761 France was not at her last gasp. Although ready to cede Canada and

---

[1] Rockingham, "Mem.," vol. i., p. 22.
[2] Lawson Grant, " La Mission de M. Bussy à Londres."
[3] Adolphus, " History of George III; " Bissett, " History of George III."
[4] Grenville Corr., vol. i., p. 342.
[5] Horace Walpole's " Letters," vol. v., p. 86.

the Mississippi trade, she clung to her fisheries, and
demanded the cession of the islands S. Pierre and
Miquelon to serve as a shelter for her fishermen. Pitt
was loth to give way ; he suspected that France was
trying to form an alliance with Spain, and feared that
she would use any cession made to her " to keep open
a door to let in Spain at our expense, as the price and
centre of naval union against England, and the only
effectual means of forming a common nursery of seamen for that purpose." [1]   Spain had no good fisheries,
and many a stalwart supporter of the Protestant succession in Great Britain grew fat through supplying
the subjects of His Catholic Majesty with the means of
abstinence. [2]

Pitt's dictatorship had ended with the accession of
George III, and as the negociations for peace proceeded it became obvious that the Chief Secretary
of State no longer ruled the Cabinet. In August, 1761,
Pitt was obliged to give way on the fishery question,
and to sanction the cession of the island of S. Pierre.
In October he resigned. When the negociations for
peace were resumed after the Spanish war, the settlement of the fishery question was entrusted to the
Duke of Bedford, who was acting as special pleni-
potentiary at the court of Versailles. Bedford no longer
held the views he had expressed in 1746. In 1761
he urged that it was useless to expect the French to
relinquish a right of fishing, " which if they do must
put a final blow to their being any longer a naval
power, though possessing a coast in the channel, and
the ocean extending from Dunkirk to the frontiers of
Spain, and from the frontiers of Spain to those of Italy."
Bedford was the only statesman of his day who treated
the fishery question from the standpoint of morality.
" To do as we would be done by," he urged, was " the

---

[1] Addit. MSS. 32927, f. 220, Pitt to Stanley, Aug. 27, 1761.
[2] Chatham Papers, 95.

most golden rule as well in what relates to the public as to private life." [1] In accordance with this policy he granted the French the islands of S. Pierre and Miquelon, and the right of fishing close to the shores of Newfoundland.

Pitt complained bitterly that these cessions were far greater than those he had so unwillingly made before the capture of Martinique or Havana, and that they gave France a grant of the whole fishery. This view of the case received some confirmation from the Board of Trade report on the preliminaries for peace, which stated with regard to S. Pierre, one of the most lucrative fishing grounds in the gulf, that the peace would make no difference, as both nations would continue to fish there as before the war. [2] Well might Pitt pronounce the peace inadequate and the cession of the fishery dangerous. The war had not been fought to secure tracts of land, but to give security to our colonists in America and prosperity to our merchants at home. It had been fought not merely to gain for ourselves, but to take from a rival, and resulted in the baptism rather than the creation of an empire. It was not the game of grab, but the old contest of French and English ; both players knew the game, but only one could count the winnings, and so it came about that while the victors secured the large coins, the vanquished kept the gold ones.

---

[1] Bedford Corr., vol. iii., p. 26.
[2] Addit. MSS. 35913.

CHAPTER V

THE WEST INDIES

" The state of the existing trade in the conquests in North America is extremely low ; the speculations as to their future trade are precarious and the prospect at the very best is remote. We stand in need of supplies, which will have an effect certain, speedy and considerable. The retaining both or even one of the considerable French islands, Martinico or Guadaloupe, will, and nothing else can, effectually answer this triple purpose. The advantage is immediate ; it is not a matter of conjecture, but of account."—Speech on the Preliminaries.

COMMERCIAL supremacy in the West Indies was the central object of Pitt's colonial policy. The capture of Martinique, the most valuable of all the French sugar islands, was his most cherished plan. He pressed it upon the Cabinet early in 1757, but received scant support from his colleagues, who were aghast at the magnitude of his designs.[1] A year later he revived his project with more success ; at home he had secured the support of his sovereign, and the capture of Louisburg had put a very different complexion on affairs abroad. Yet it was not till after a hard fight in the Council that Pitt secured the adoption of his plan. Newcastle grew querulous when he found that the King and Pitt thought the war must last another year, and were " for driving the French out of America and for getting other parts besides." Lord Anson declared he did not relish the Martinico project ; but Pitt was firm, and declared that if every other

---

[1] Addit. MSS. 32997, f. 258, Newcastle Papers, Claremont, Sept. 7, 1757. " Business with Lord Hardwicke, Mr. Pitt's Suggestion to winter a Squadron in North America ; and possibly to make an attempt from thence in the winter upon St. Domingo or Martinico."

expedition were stopped those to the West Indies and Africa should be adequately supported.[1] There were, indeed, many points of resemblance between Pitt's African and West Indian policies. In both he warred for and upon trade; in both his victories were designed to secure a market from which his countrymen were being driven. In 1758 the position of the British colonists in the Antilles was a grave one. France owned the two most considerable islands, Martinique and Guadaloupe, whose excellent harbours give anchorage to her men-of-war during the hurricane season, and afforded shelter to the swarms of privateers who preyed upon her enemy's commerce. Nor was it merely in time of war that the French islands were formidable. At the beginning of the Seven Years' War our sugar colonies were suffering severely from French competition. The French advantage at that time was not due to one of those fluctuations of good fortune, or rather temporary absences of earthquake, pestilence, or other calamity, which caused West Indian prosperity to be spasmodic and difficult to estimate.[2] In 1756 the French colonists had many constant and substantial advantages over their rivals. The British West Indian planters made great quantities of their sugar into rum and sent it to England, but France protected herself against colonial spirits which might interfere with her native brandy, consequently sugars were cheaper in the French islands than in the British, and the New England colonies preferred to trade with the former. By the returns of this trade, which was fostered by the French governor at Martinique, the French islands secured provisions and the hardware and wood necessary for the manufacture and packing of their sugars.[3] The greater fertility

---

[1] Addit. MSS. 32998, f. 171.

[2] *Cf.* C. M. H., vol. vii., chap. 2. "The French in America." By Mary Bateson.

[3] Cunningham, "History of Industry and Commerce, Modern Times," part. i., p. 479.

of their islands and the lower duties they paid enabled the French to produce the same commodities as the English in greater plenty, and to undersell them in all foreign markets. Their privateers also annoyed British trading vessels who sailed near the coasts of Martinique or Guadaloupe.[1]

Barbadoes, the chief of the English Windward Islands, possessed no adequate harbour, nor was this deficiency supplied by the Leeward Group, Antigua and her dependencies, S. Christopher and the Virgin Islands. The latter were comparatively unfertile, and it was even argued that France had gained by ceding S. Christopher to Great Britain in 1713, and concentrating her forces at Martinique and Guadaloupe. S. Lucia, Dominica, Grenada, S. Vincent, and Tobago were nominally neutral, but all except the last were settled and governed by the French, who also traded with the natives, who lived in a blissful state of anarchy at Tobago. The Governor of Martinique gave an old chief of Tobago who visited him the title of General, which pleased him much at the time, though he afterwards found it added little to his dignity at home. When Captain Tyrrel secured the island for Great Britain in 1758, he found nine French families living in Tobago, who assured him they had chosen that place of residence because there they could find all the necessities of life and liberty, both of which they would be deprived of in any civilised country.[2] French influence was gaining on all sides, and every year the British colonies grew weaker as their rivals closed round and cut them off from one another. A lively sense of their danger induced the West Indian colonists to co-operate heartily with Pitt in his designs upon Martinique and Guadaloupe. The support they gave

---

[1] C.O. 28, 32, Governor Pinfold to the Lords of Trade, June 1, 1762, " The Condition of Trade before the War."
[2] C.O. 152, 46. " State of Tobago." Enclosed in Pinfold's letter to Pitt of Jan. 7, 1758.

furnishes some evidence of their economic conditions at the time.

In October, 1758, Pitt wrote to Governor Pinfold of Barbadoes informing him of the intended attack upon Martinique, and desiring him to give all possible assistance to Major-General Hopson, and if possible supply him with men and horses. Governor Thomas, who was in command of the Leeward Islands, was directed to enable a detachment of the 38th regiment of foot, on duty at Antigua, to join the expedition with all possible speed.[1] The men of Barbadoes were very sensible of the protection which Pitt's cruisers had afforded to their trade during the last year, nor were they unwilling to help themselves. They had already fitted out a brigantine which could pursue the smaller French privateers better than the men-of-war, and escape more easily in slack winds by the use of oars.[2] When General Hopson arrived with Pitt's despatches, the Governor summoned his council and assembly, who voted a bonus of 20s. to every man who would embark. But it was found impossible to procure tents and other necessaries on the island at short notice, and the General contented himself with a supply of negroes, who were to act instead of the " Beasts of Draught " desired by Pitt.[3]

Governor Thomas proved more successful. He at once despatched the regulars with ammunition and provisions for two months ; and in a letter to Pitt, of Feb. 17, waxed eloquent over the hoped-for conquest of Martinique. " The conquest and settlement of this island," he declared, " will be an additional jewel to the crown, and add strength to the Leeward Islands by drawing our force into a narrower compass from Anguilla, Spanish Town, and other worthless Virgin Islands." [4]

---

[1] Col. Corr., vol. i., p. 366.
[2] C.O. 28, 31, Pinfold to the Lords of Trade, Jan. 7, 1758.
[3] C.O. 152, 46, Pinfold to Pitt, Jan. 17, 1759.
[4] C.O. 152, 46.

The attack on Martinique failed, though the inhabitants were reduced to sore straits by the blockade, and forced to kill the cattle which worked their sugar-mills.[1] Hopson next turned his attentions to Guadaloupe, an alternative proposed by Pitt in his instructions. The General asked Governor Thomas to raise troops of whites and blacks for this expedition. As it was not in his power to compel the owners of slaves to part with them, the Governor summoned his council and assembly, who voted 300 negroes. At first Governor Thomas despaired of raising white men, as most of the adventurous spirits of the island were already on board her numerous privateers—which service was very attractive " to the lower classes of people," as the plunder they took was their own.[2] Finally, however, Antigua and S. Christopher between them sent 150 white men and 460 blacks. The gentlemen of the islands also subscribed £1,000 in a week to supply the troops with cattle, sheep, poultry, wine, and spices, and £800 for raising and clothing the white volunteers.[3]

By the capture of Guadaloupe, the men of the Leeward Islands felt fully repaid for the great efforts they had made. Their Governor sent hearty congratulations to the Secretary of State, hoped that France would now be forced to consent to the division of the neutral islands, and above all that England would keep Guadaloupe. He declared that this island, " from its situation and fertility if kept by His Majesty at the peace, and settled principally by British subjects, would add greatly to the security of the Leeward Islands, increase the revenue, lower the price of sugar, supply in a great part the home consumption of coffee, cocoa, and cotton, and very much contribute to the

---

[1] C.O. 152, 46.
[2] *Ibid.*, Feb. 28, 1759.
[3] *Ibid.*, April 21, 1759.

safety of the British commerce both to the Leeward Islands and to Jamaica." Governor Thomas affirmed he was emboldened to give his opinion on these matters of state, because he knew that Pitt was always disposed to give a fair hearing to everything that concerned the welfare of his country.[1]

Guadaloupe was a most potential conquest. It consisted of two islands. Guadaloupe proper contained 128 large sugar plantations, besides smaller ones for cotton and coffee, and was inhabited by 5,489 white men and 16,298 negroes, not counting those under fourteen or over sixty years of age, who paid no duty to the king. Grandterre, which was separated from Guadaloupe by a salt river, was one continuous plain, with little hills here and there on which the houses were built. It contained 190 sugar-works, whose proprietors owned 17,566 able-bodied slaves. The two islands together exceeded Martinique in size and value.[2] An immense amount of French money was locked up in Guadaloupe. It was computed that a capital of £30,000 was necessary to start a sugar plantation of average size, that is 900 acres, though even if the estate were smaller the capital employed was not much less, as buildings were the chief expense. The mill alone cost over £1,000, and then the planter had to provide a boiling house, a curing house, a distillery, stables for his mules, a dwelling house for his overseer, storehouses, hospitals for sick negroes, a prison for unruly ones, " a doctor's shop," and workshops for his carpenters, coopers, wheelwrights, and smith. The stock of the planta tions usually consisted, according to the classification of the day, of negroes, steers, and mules. This varied according to the size of the estate and the power used for the mill, which might be water, wind, or oxen.[3]

---

[1] C.O. 152, 46, May 29, 1759.
[2] C.O. 110, 2, Governor Dalrymple to Egremont, Feb. 16, 1762.
[3] Bryan Edwards, " History of the West Indies," vol. ii., p. 248.

The Islands of the Saints capitulated after the reduction of Guadaloupe ; their only products were provisions and a little coffee and cotton. It was estimated that the French annual revenue from Guadaloupe and her dependencies had been 309,000 livres, and their expenses 147,230 livres, which left a balance of 161,770 livres, exclusive of a duty of 3½ per cent. paid on all produce on importation from these islands into any of the ports of France.[1] The terms of capitulation secured the customary revenue of the islands to Great Britain, and prohibited any trade except with England.

Guadaloupe was lucky in her English Governors. The first was Colonel Crump, who had considerable knowledge of the West Indies, and had the welfare of the islanders at heart.[2] He did his utmost to make them feel that they had gained by the change of masters. This could hardly fail to be the case. Under French rule the interests of Guadaloupe had been subordinated to those of Martinique, the centre of all the French commerce in the West Indies. One English memorialist, who urged the British Government to attack Martinique, spoke of that island as the root which nourished her branches.[3] But Guadaloupe, S. Lucia, and Mariegalante regarded her rather as the greedy body which they had to support. A planter from one of these islands had to send his produce to Martinique, land it, roll it up to the magazines of his factor there, and pay 5 per cent. commission for the sale. Even this was not the worst of his trials, for when he took his payment in the European commodities he required, 100 per cent. did not always satisfy his rapacious commissioner.[4] The colonists were delighted to be

---

[1] C.O. 110, 2, Dalrymple to Egremont, Feb. 16, 1762. *Cf.* Col. Corr., vol. ii., p. 175, where the figures given are higher.
[2] Col. Corr., vol. ii., p. 102.
[3] Chat. MSS. 98.
[4] C.O. 110, 2.

able to send their sugars straight to Europe. Some difficulty arose over their coffee, which was an article whose importation into Great Britain was forbidden, but the prohibition was waived in favour of the new acquisitions.

Governor Crump did his utmost to hasten the rebuilding of the houses and factories which had suffered in the reduction of the island. He was succeeded by Colonel Dalrymple, who carried on the work in the same spirit. He sent convoys every six months to protect the merchantmen on their way to Great Britain, and some rough idea of the progress of the colony under his charge may be gained from the half-yearly custom-house returns. Those for the six months from February 1 to July 31, 1761, included 19,053 hogsheads of sugar, 5,476 hogsheads of molasses, 2,571,821 pounds of coffee, 1,769 bales of cotton, 304 hogsheads of rum, 830 hogsheads of cocoa, 28,210 pounds of allspice, and seventy-nine casks of ginger. When this return is compared with those of 1754 and 1757, two of the best years under French rule, when the island only entered 17,500 hogsheads of sugar at the custom-house and other things in proportion, it is clear that the produce of the island had more than doubled. A plentiful supply of slaves and improved cultivation had contributed to this prosperity.[1]

In the peace negociations of 1761 Pitt reluctantly consented to the restitution of Guadaloupe as the price of Minorca. He declared afterwards that he had been overruled in the council, and hinted at a secret influence; but at that date many of the old Whigs counselled moderate demands. The Duke of Newcastle was in despair over the state of the exchequer, and Lord Hardwicke was influenced by his representations of the serious financial position.[2] In fact, in 1761

---

[1] C.O. 110, 2, Dalrymple to Egremont, Oct. 29, 1761.
[2] Addit. MSS. 33000, f. 137.

Great Britain was suffering the strain of the war, and had not within her grasp all those materials for a solid edifice of a lasting peace whose design was maturing in the great empire-builder's mind.

By the beginning of August Pitt was convinced that peace could only be gained by war, and reverted to his early plan for the reduction of Martinique. On August 5 he wrote to the Governors of Barbadoes and the Leeward Islands, giving notice of his plans, and requesting them to raise men, cattle, provisions, and refreshments of any kind that their governments were able to furnish.[1]   At home his preparations were carried on with the usual secrecy and despatch. Admiral Rodney was given command of the expedition, and promised the aid of troops from Belleisle and North America. The whole force was to reach Martinique by the end of October at the latest.[2] Pitt resigned on October 2.   On October 5 the Duke of Newcastle made a memorandum : " To get immediately all the letters and papers from Mr. Pitt's office, relating to the attempts on Martinico and all other projects, as to the carrying them into execution, or under deliberation, what orders have been given, or remain to be given, and what additional force ought to be sent.   To hasten away all the troops, ships, and officers designed for these succours." [3]   The preparations for the Martinico expedition were completed almost before the Secretary of State had had time to peruse the paper from Mr. Pitt's office.   On October 9 Rodney reported to the Admiralty that he was ready to sail.[4]

Meanwhile great preparations had been made in the British West Indies. This time Barbadoes was

---

[1] Col. Corr., vol. ii., p. 456.   For Pitt's naval and military plans for the West Indies, 1760-1761, see B. Williams, " Pitt," vol. ii., pp. 20-21.
[2] Col. Corr., vol. ii., p. 459.
[3] Addit. MSS. 32929, f. 66.
[4] Rodney Papers, 7. Rodney to the Lords of the Admiralty, Oct. 9, 1761.

determined not to let any material difficulties hamper the expression of her loyalty. The early notice that Pitt had given of his project and the possibility of getting supplies from Guadaloupe also removed some of the difficulties that had been overwhelming in 1759.[1] Governor Pinfold received Pitt's letter on October 6, hastily drafted a Bill for the enlistment of troops, summoned his council, who approved his plan and advised that it should be submitted to the assembly. The assembly met the same evening and appointed committees of both Houses. On the next day the Bill became law.[2] It provided for the enrolment of ten companies of foot soldiers, each to consist of fifty private men, one drummer, three corporals, and two sergeants, under the command of a captain, a lieutenant, and an ensign. Each man was to receive 20s., and to be furnished with a uniform, suit of "Oznabigs cloaths," two shirts, a hat and a pair of shoes. The private's pay 2s. 6d. a day, the corporal's 3s. 1½d. The sergeant was to receive 3s. 9d., the ensign 7s. 6d., the lieutenant 10s., the captain 15s., the surgeon the same, and his mate 5s. less. Prisoners who were confined for debts of less than £300 were given the chance of enlistment and freedom. But the raising of a sufficient force was not left entirely to voluntary effort, for one clause of the Bill enacted :

" that any man who not having wherewith to maintain himself lives idle without employment and refuses to work for the usual and common wages ; or who leaves his wife and children, whereby they become chargeable to any parish ; or who wanders abroad and begs, may be compelled to serve His Majesty in the said Company by any two Justices of Peace who are hereby required and empowered to commit such persons to the common gaol of this island to be disposed of amongst the said Company by his Excellency or the Commander-in-Chief for the time being."

---

[1] C.O. 152, 46, Governor Pinfold to Pitt, Nov. 15, 1761.
[2] *Ibid.*, Pinfold to Pitt, Oct. 28, 1761.

Provision was also made that an annuity should be paid to the widow or children of any private or non-commissioned officer who was killed in the expedition, and compensation given to men who were disabled for life. The assembly also voted 600 negroes, which the Governor explained to Pitt were to supply the place of the cattle he had requested, but which the island was unable to furnish. Every person who possessed thirty or more slaves was forced to contribute one able-bodied man slave, and one more from every 100 he possessed exclusive of the first thirty. " Each slave to be provided with a backed bill, a hoe fixed, a Baskett; and cloathed with a good jackett, a pair of Trouzes and a hat or Monmouth cap." Their masters were to deliver them to certain persons at an appointed place where they would be valued. From the day they were delivered the master was to receive 1s. 10½d. for each slave, and to be given compensation if the slave returned sick or wounded. " And in case any of the said slaves shall not be returned at all, either by reason of death or be run away so as not to be found," the owner was to be given the full value of the slave. A fine of £20 was to be inflicted for every slave that was not sent. An embargo was placed on all ships and boats in the ports of the island to prevent the news of the proposed expedition from being carried to the enemy.

This plan succeeded so admirably that when Rodney arrived in November he found 590 white men, including officers, clothed, armed and furnished with camp equipage. The men were in companies ready to embark at an hour's warning, and had been constantly exercised for two months before his arrival. The admiral was also presented with " 600 able-bodied negroes to draw the cannon and to be employed as he shall direct." [1] Antigua supplied 300 slaves, but

---

[1] Rodney Papers, 8.

the Governor regretted he could raise no white men, as the islands under his care were "so weak and disjoined."[1]

Rodney found that the West Indian colonists were good marksmen and extremely useful as rangers.[2] After the reduction of Martinique, S. Lucia, and the Grenadoes, and the declaration of war with Spain, Barbadoes helped His Majesty's forces materially by receiving numbers of prisoners and sick and wounded. Both classes of guests taxed the resources of the islanders severely. The Governor reported, "The prisoners both French and Spanish behave well, and have been guilty of no disturbance of the public peace, but the uneasiness of the inhabitants and the sollicitations of the prisoners to get away occasion me a great deal of trouble, which I make no doubt you will remove as soon as possible."[3]

The sick proved even more difficult to accommodate, and were always overflowing the hospital. It was also found difficult to provide nurses for them. Negro women were tried, but being "a very sleepy indolent sort of people" frequently neglected their charges, and always slept soundly when placed on night duty. After 1761 the strain on the West Indian colonies was severe. They suffered much from the enemies' privateers, were in constant fear of attacks, and could only send their produce to England when the Admiral chose to send a convoy. But they bore their discomforts loyally, and lived in hopes of a peace which should give them lasting security.

Rodney was delighted with the capture of Martinique, and could not praise the harbour and roads of Fort Royal sufficiently; he declared that the former was the best and safest harbour in all these parts of the West Indies, and "the road without it one of

[1] C.O. 152, 47, Thomas to Rodney, Dec. 4, 1761.
[2] Rodney Papers, 8, Rodney to Sir Jeffrey Amherst, Dec. 4, 1761.
[3] *Ibid.*, Pinfold to Rodney, May 3, 1762.

F

the noblest in the world." [1]   But the inhabitants of
Martinique were none too pleased with their change
of masters.   Their terms of capitulation were much
harsher than those of Guadaloupe, and forced them to
quarter the troops, lodge the officers, and furnish ham-
mocks, firewood, and hospitals.   Their trade suffered
severely from the ruin of their works caused by the
siege, and as under British rule Martinique ceased to
be the staple for the Guadaloupe trade, she lost in
proportion as her rival gained.   Governor Rufane
regulated the Martinique trade by the same rules that
Dalrymple had drawn up for Guadaloupe.   Great
care was taken both to improve the quality of the
exports and to confine them to Great Britain.   Every
bale of cotton was marked with the name of the
planter and the parish in which he lived.   The
adulteration of sugars with sand or inferior sugar
was guarded against.   Every cask was carefully branded.
Weights were tested once a year. [2]   Half-yearly convoys
took the produce home.   This consisted of clayed or
refined sugar, Muscovado or half-manufactured sugar,
rum, molasses, cocoa, coffee, cotton, spices, tobacco,
tortoiseshell, syrup, lime juice, rice, sweetmeats, and
snuff.   The duties on these from April 6 to July 5,
1762, amounted to £2,868 11s. 9½d., and from July
to October they produced £3,690 13s. 8½d. [3]   The
excellent supply of running water which was peculiar
to Martinique had a definite commercial value.
There were 116 water-mills on the island at the time
of the conquest, each of which was reckoned by the
English to be worth two oxen or wind-mills.   The
Governor found it very difficult to confine the commerce of the island to Great Britain.   Sugar was

---

[1] Rodney Papers, 8, Rodney to the Commissioners of the Navy,
Feb. 24, 1762.
[2] C.O. 110, 1, Regulations received from General Dalrymple, July 22,
1761.
[3] C.O. 166, 2.

made all the year round, and a great quantity was shipped to France through the Dutch at St. Eustatius. The English colonists in North America, who had long carried on an extensive illicit commerce with Martinique, petitioned to be allowed to import sugar and coffee. They represented that the West Indian Islands depended almost entirely on them for flour, pork, gammon, staves, hoops, and corn ; and that the proper returns for these imports were molasses, rum, cocoa, coffee, and sugar. The Government regulations cut them off from the two last articles, and as there was only a little very bad rum made in the French islands, there remained only molasses, which was of little value compared with the cargoes imported. As all the British West Indian Islands were allowed to export sugar to North America on paying the enumerated duties, the Governor granted what he considered a very reasonable request.[1] In fact, it was obvious to those on the spot that it was impossible to prevent commercial intercourse between the colonies of the mainland and the most considerable West Indian Islands, be they French or English.

Meanwhile Guadaloupe had continued to flourish, and while under British rule gained a permanent superiority over Martinique. Governor Dalrymple had written to Egremont on December 6, 1761 : " Give me leave, my lord, to inform you that by the resignation of Mr. Pitt I have lost my best friend and protector, but as a constant application to my duty was my chief introduction to him, so I doubt not but a strict attention to the same will also recommend me to your lordship's protection." [2] When rumours of the proposed terms of peace reached the industrious governor in the summer of 1762, he wrote to the Secretary of State and urged him to remember that

---

[1] C.O. 166, 2, Rufane to Egremont, July 19, 1762.
[2] C.O. 110, 2.

too small a value had been set on Guadaloupe in the negociations of the previous year, and reminded him that since then the revenue of the island had increased considerably. He also wrote to the Secretary of the Board of Trade that he was sorry to hear it even suspected that France was to reap all the fruit of our labours, but philosophically consoled himself with the reflection that they had been very advantageous to us in the meantime.[1] Indeed it was held by some of the best informed among the English statesmen that without the advantage we gained from our West Indian conquests we could not have borne the con-tinued expense of the war.[2]

In his great speech on the preliminaries for peace on December 9, 1762, Pitt severely censured the cession of Guadaloupe and Martinique ; and in a few terse phrases outlined his great imperial plan.

" We stand in need of supplies which will have an effect certain, speedy and considerable. The retaining both, or even one of the considerable French islands, Martinique or Guadaloupe, will, and nothing else can, effectually answer this triple purpose. The advantage is immediate, it is not a matter of conjecture but of account. The trade with these conquests is of the most lucrative nature, and of the most considerable extent ; the number of ships employed by it are a great resource to our maritime power ; and, what is of equal weight, all that we gain on this system is made fourfold to us by the loss which ensues to France. But our conquests in North America are of very little detriment to the commerce of France. On the West Indian Scheme of acquisition, our gain and her loss go hand in hand. He insisted upon the obvious connection of this trade with that of the colonies in North America, and with our commerce to the coast of Africa. The African trade would be augmented, which, with that of North America, would all centre in Great Britain. But if the islands are all

---

[1] C.O. 110, 2, Dalrymple to Wood, Oct. 17, 1762.
[2] Addit. MSS. 33000. Even Newcastle thought that after the reduction of Martinique the war could have been carried on another year.

restored, a great part of the benefit of the colony trade must redound to those who were lately our enemies and must always be our rivals. Though we had retained either Martinique or Guadaloupe, or even both these islands, our conquests were such that there was still abundant matter left to display our moderation."[1]

It has been pointed out that in the middle of the eighteenth century there were two distinct theories with regard to colonial values. The older school of economists regarded a colony as a source of supply, but the more modern thinkers, who realised that the manufactures of Great Britain were fast becoming more important than her agriculture, desired a colonial market for home industries. The former school had long regarded the West Indies as ideal colonies, the latter were turning their attention to the rapidly increasing population of the North American plantations. It has been argued that in the early negociations, when Pitt agreed to cede Guadaloupe rather than Canada, he acted in accordance with the theories of the newer school, but that in his criticism of the peace in 1762 he reverted to the old idea that a colony should be valued as a source of supply.[2] In reality Pitt saw further than any economists of his day. They showered tracts upon him showing the comparative value of Canada and Guadaloupe. He insisted on their obvious connection. History has proved what he could only predict. It has always been found impossible to prevent trade between the mainland of America and the West Indian Islands. Pitt knew that our own inferior sugar islands were daily becoming more unable to meet the growing demands of the Northern plantations, and that the retention of one or both of the considerable islands would secure to Great Britain the trade that must go there in any case.

---

[1] " Thackeray," vol. ii., p. 17.
[2] G. L. Beer, " British Colonial Policy," p. 136.

Indeed, the peace was hardly signed, before the
Governor of Martinique issued commercial regulations
permitting trade under certain conditions between the
island under his charge and the British North American
colonies.[1]

Pitt has often been accused of being too grasping.
His most recent biographer has urged that his demands
were dictated by a consuming hatred of France.[2]
It is certain that his colonial policy was inspired by the
great passion of his life, but this was fear rather than
hatred.   He feared France because he understood the
natural character of her resources and the artificial
basis of those of Great Britain.   All students of the
history of France must be struck by her magnificent
power of recovery.[3]   The strength of our great ally
to-day is a curious comment upon the Napoleonic
struggle and the Franco-Prussian War.   Pitt had
noted the speedy recuperation of French finances
after the War of the Austrian Succession, and believed
that the only way to keep England's rival in bounds
was to confine her to the continent.[4]

It is sometimes urged that even if Great Britain
withdrew all political control from her oversea
dependencies she might yet keep the essential parts
of her empire, if an efficient navy and wise regulations protected her trade routes.   This is no eighteenth century view; but Pitt had a vision of a stream
of commerce flowing from the various ends of a vast
empire.   Great Britain was to be the brains of this
body politic, and the West Indies the heart through
which the life-blood flowed.   In vain he dwelt upon
the obvious connection between the trade of the mainland, the islands and our possessions in West Africa.

---

[1] C.O. 388, 95.
[2] Basil Williams, " Pitt," vol. ii., p. 86.
[3] Holland Rose, " Life of Napoleon."
[4] Raynal, " History of the West Indies."

By the peace of Paris, France received back Martinique and Guadaloupe in infinitely better condition than when she surrendered them. The speedy recovery of her finances and marine enabled her to give decisive help to the rebellious colonies of Great Britain less than twenty years after the day when she lay at our mercy.

CHAPTER VI

" The popularity of Pitt was hardly less in Ireland than in England. On his retirement from office the merchants and traders of Dublin presented him with an address expressing their enthusiastic admiration for his career. The citizens of Cork erected a marble statue of him in their Exchange."—Lecky, " History of Ireland," vol. ii., p. 69.

THE first office held by Pitt was an Irish one. On March 6, 1746, he received the high-sounding title of Vice-Treasurer and Receiver General and Pay-master General of all His Majesty's Revenues, and Treasurer of War for the kingdom of Ireland.[1] The post was almost a sinecure ; every week his subordinates in Ireland sent him the accounts and £50 for himself. Pitt was sufficiently interested to preserve an historical account of the office among his private papers, but he quitted it in May, on becoming Pay-master General, without taking the oath or visiting Ireland.[2]

Ten years later, as Secretary of State, he was obliged to study Irish affairs more closely. The economic position of Ireland in 1756 was an apt illustration of the fallacies of the old colonial system. Technically Ireland was a plantation, and the Protestant landowners were colonists whose interests were wholly subservient to those of the mother country. Their duty was to govern, and if possible convert the Roman Catholic aborigines, and to keep Ireland safe from foreign

---

[1] Ruville, " Life of Pitt," vol. i., p. 266.
[2] Chatham Papers, 84.

invasion.[1] The policy of commercial restraint, successfully pursued for two centuries, had left Ireland with two main resources, agriculture and the linen industry. Intensive agriculture was depressed by the exorbitant profits charged by the middlemen, who stood between cotton occupiers and absentee landlords ; but grazing was very profitable, and Ireland exported large quantities of beef, pork, and butter. The markets of England and her colonies were closed to the sister kingdom, but she did a considerable trade by victualling French ships. The Irish linen industry was consistently encouraged by England. But what was given with one hand was taken away with the other, for all Irish enterprise was hampered by a disgraceful pension list. Out of her slender resources Ireland had to provide for men who had never set foot on her shores, and for women who should certainly have been beyond the pale.

Pitt brought no special sympathies to the study of Irish affairs, but he dealt justly with those that came within his province, and gradually evolved an Irish policy which was far in advance of the views held by most statesmen of his day. As Secretary of State, his attention was drawn towards Ireland as a part of the British Isles, capable of supplying men and provisions for the Imperial war and a vulnerable spot in the line of British defence. In 1757 men were urgently needed both for foreign service and home defence. Pitt wrote repeatedly to the Duke of Bedford, then Lieutenant Governor for Ireland, urging him to raise troops.[2] Bedford was not unsuccessful, but he failed to satisfy Pitt, who drafted away the Irish companies for foreign service as soon as they were completed,

---

[1] Cf. Lecky's " History of Ireland," vol. ii., p. 52 ; " Cambridge Modern History," vol. vi., chap. xiv. ; " Two Centuries of Irish History," part i., by Dr. Sullivan.
[2] S.P.F., Ireland, 415, Pitt to Bedford, Jan. 25, 1757.

leaving Bedford in despair for the safety of the kingdom under his charge.[1]

The position of an eighteenth-century Lord Lieutenant in Ireland was one of the greatest difficulty. The Irish Parliament only sat every two years, and the Lord Lieutenant usually only resided in Ireland while Parliament was sitting. In his absence the King's business was undertaken by three Lord Justices, of whom the Speaker and Primate were frequently two, and a great landowner the third. These "undertakers," as they were popularly called, were the real rulers of Ireland, and a Lord Lieutenant who thwarted their plans soon discovered that his own measures were rejected by Parliament with contempt. The rule of the undertakers was universally corrupt. The very limited resources of Ireland were annually squandered in jobs, which under the name of improvements loaded every money bill.[2] The Duke of Bedford was an able man of undoubted integrity. He tried to play off the would-be undertakers against one another, and fought valiantly against many a job that was afterwards laid to his credit. But he was often betrayed by a hasty temper, a warm heart, and prejudiced advisers. By nature tolerant and humane, Bedford was only too willing to follow Pitt's instructions, and try to meet the Irish difficulties with " gentle healing measures." Yet he was far too acute an observer to allow his own inclination to blind him to real danger. Directly he arrived in Ireland he saw that the distempered state of the nation required an iron tonic rather than a cooling draught ; and begged that the forces of Ireland might be augmented.[3] But Pitt was playing a game of bluff, and Ireland was a royal card he was obliged to leave uncovered. In

---

[1] Bedford Corr., vol. ii., p. 360, Bedford to Pitt, Aug. 29, 1758.
[2] " The Irish Parliament," ed. W. Hunt.
[3] Bedford Corr., vol. iii., pp. 285, 287, 327, 360.

1759 he received information that Marshal Conflans was preparing for an attack on Ireland, and urged the Lord Lieutenant to hasten the recruiting and make every possible preparation to repel an invasion. Bedford declared that he had every confidence in the zeal of the Irish Protestants, but confessed that the army was weak and undisciplined, and begged again for reinforcements from England.

It was one of those desperate cases in which it would have been cruel to be sympathetic, and Pitt replied with the stinging retort that the Protestant zeal of Ireland, though undoubted, was singularly inefficient. He maintained that the kingdom was able to repel invasion, suggested that the linen manufacturers were unwilling to leave the looms, and contrasted their conduct with that of the English militia who had been out through haymaking and harvest.[1]   In conclusion, he noted that the city of London had raised more men that year than the kingdom of Ireland. Pitt made the same invidious comparison in the House of Commons, and told the Irishmen present to send his message to their countrymen. They hated him for sacrificing the pride of a kingdom to civic self-esteem,[2] but the gibe did its work ; when the Lord Lieutenant informed the Irish Parliament of the danger of invasion he met with a liberal response to his appeal for help. The Earl of Drogheda immediately offered to raise a complete regiment of light dragoons of 474 men, and to provide them with " levy money, swords, buff accoutrements, boots, saddles and bridle furniture, with drums, standards and all other necessaries, except horses and arms, which are articles exceeding the bounds of a private fortune."[3] Several Irish gentlemen raised companies at their own expense. Altogether, in 1759, Ireland raised six new regiments and a

[1] Bedford Corr., vol. iii., Nov. 2, 1759, Pitt to Bedford.
[2] " State of Ireland," Hely Hutchinson.
[3] S.P., Ireland, 416, Bedford to Pitt, Nov. 12, 1759.

troop, which was the more generous when it is considered, as Bedford reminded Pitt, that there were very
few men resident in Ireland whose wealth could be
compared with that of the London city men.

The strain was too much for Ireland. In November
three of the principal banks stopped payment. One
of them was owned by Mr. Clements, the deputy
paymaster; and other members of the government
were concerned in the business. Bedford had foreseen,
and tried to prevent this financial crisis,[1] but it was
inevitable. Ireland was habitually without sufficient
specie to carry on her ordinary commerce. This
condition of affairs was largely due to the unrestrained
system of private banking and issue of notes. Ireland
was peculiarly unsuited for a paper currency, being
too poor to consume her own productions; her trade
was chiefly with foreign nations. Thus bad money
quickly drove out good, and any extra drain produced
a dearth. The banks also invested their capital in
land and mortgages, securities which could not be
realised when an invasion threatened.[2]

Bank failures were common enough in Dublin, but
none the less distressing to a poverty-stricken com-
munity. When Mr. Clements' bank stopped payment
there was a tremendous outcry. Several riots took
place, members of Parliament were prevented by the
mob from entering the House; some were dragged
from their coaches, very roughly handled, and made to
take an oath to be true to the interests of Ireland.
The Lord Lieutenant was accused of " diabolical
attempts at union," and challenged to fight a duel.
In his report of the riot to the Secretary of State,
Bedford made no mention of the economic causes of
the disturbance, but put it down to Papists and French
emissaries.[3] These useful red herrings did not

---

[1] Bedford Corr., vol. iii., p. 389, Bedford to Pitt, Nov. 1, 1759.
[2] Woburn MSS. 67, ff. 2, 5, 19.
[3] S.P., Ireland, 416, Bedford to Pitt, Dec. 5, 1759.

prevent Pitt from tracking down the true offenders. He was not solely dependent on his official correspondence for his information on Irish affairs, and knew that most of the rioters were Protestant weavers who had suffered severely from the financial crisis caused by the speculations of government officials. For the latter Pitt had no mercy, and he desired Bedford " To reflect seriously how far most unwarrantable money dealings by persons in places of High trust in His Majesty's service in Ireland (dealings universally considered here as full of scandal and reproach to Servants of Government) may not have contributed not a little to have extinguished in the minds of the multitude their respect for government itself." [1] The Lord Lieutenant defended his underlings with more warmth than discretion, and urged that they had only done what was customary. Precedent was on Bedford's side, but public opinion was with Pitt. Even the Duke of Newcastle was shocked, and expressed a very general view of the case when he said, " I doubt not, but private persons may in time recover their money, but my objection is that persons in such high stations, concerned or thought to be so, with the publick money should avowedly and in their own names set up a publick bank, and put themselves upon a level with and subject to the same chances, failings and misfortunes, that common bankers are." [2]

Although Pitt might realise there was cause for discontent, he never condoned rebellion. On this occasion he urged Bedford to use every endeavour to bring the rioters who had outraged the majesty of Parliament to condign punishment. Some arrests had been made at the time of the disturbances, but most of the prisoners turned out to have been harmless spectators. Nor was it easy to collect information as to the real ringleaders. Many witnesses were

---

[1] S.P., Ireland, 416, Pitt to Bedford, Dec. 20, 1759.
[2] Addit. MSS. 32900, Newcastle to Rigby, Dec. 20, 1759.

ready to swear that they had seen a man in a brown
coat beating a drum, which was the signal for the
riot, but although they were very positive as to the
drum and the coat, not one of them could describe
the man.[1] After some investigations, Bedford reported that he had now learned that the majority of
the rioters were New Light Presbyterians, or Twadlers,
whose republican tenets made them at least as dangerous
as the Papists. If it were the Lord Lieutenant's
object to divert the Secretary of State's wrath from
himself he chose his scapegoats badly, for in his reply
to this despatch Pitt expressed great concern that his
Grace should think there was cause to consider any
one class of Presbyterians in Ireland averse to English
government, and therefore at least, equally with
Papists, to be guarded against, and continued : " I
am not very particularly acquainted with the dis-
tinctive tenets of the sect among them mentioned by
your Grace, but it highly imports Government to
reflect however blameworthy the too rigid adherence
of the Presbyterians to some things may be justly
thought, in comparison with the excellence of the
Church of England, that nevertheless the Presbyterians
must ever deserve to be considered in opposition to
the Church of Rome, as a very valuable branch of the
reformation ; and that with regard to their civil
principle that respectable body have in all times
shewed themselves both in England and Ireland firm
and zealous supporters of the Glorious Revolution
under King William and of the present happy establishment." In conclusion, Bedford was urged to
exert every means in his power " to encourage and
improve the spirit which manifests itself among the
King's Protestant subjects in Ireland to take arms in
defence of all that is dear to them." [2]

---

[1] S.P., Ireland, 416.
[2] S.P.F., Ireland, 418, Pitt to Bedford, Jan. 5, 1760.

Bedford made strenuous efforts to carry out his instructions, and succeeded in spite of enormous difficulties. The Protestant population of Ireland, from whom alone the recruits were supposed to be drawn, was sparse. The linen industry of the North was Ireland's chief source of revenue, and Bedford was naturally reluctant to call out the Ulster weavers. Nor did the Irish recruiting parties have a free field. Unauthorised bands recruited in Ireland for the English regiments and the East India Company showed its usual enterprise by sending a well-known English prize-fighter, resplendent in the uniform of a marine, to capture Irish heads and hearts.[1] Bedford made several valuable suggestions as to the best means of providing for the defence of Ireland. One was that " people of a better sort " who had refused to join the infantry might be willing to enrol themselves in a troop of horse.[2] Another idea of the Lord Lieutenant's, which was carried out with marked success, was that gentlemen who lived in Catholic districts should be encouraged to raise companies of marines without enquiring too closely into the religion of their recruits.[3] Pitt warmly approved Bedford's initiative, and promised him liberal financial aid from the mother country.

Hawkes' victory over Conflans had secured Great Britain from any serious French invasion, but early in 1760 Irishmen were given an opportunity of proving their loyalty and valour. On February 21 three large ships were sighted off Carrickfergus. They were a French expedition under the command of M. de Flobert, a man of considerable military knowledge and eloquence. His second in command was the renowned M. Thurot, a brave man of very varied fortunes and experiences. For many years he was

---

[1] S.P., Ireland, 416.
[2] *Ibid.*, 418.
[3] *Ibid.*

engaged in smuggling between France, Ireland, and
the Isle of Man. He had a thorough knowledge of
the Irish coast, and was naturally well acquainted with
Irish industries and commerce. At a council of war
he strongly advised that Carrickfergus should be left
and an immediate attack made upon Belfast, the third
city of the kingdom, which he knew would be an easy
plunder. But Flobert, who considered that it would
be a grave tactical error to leave a fortified place like
Carrickfergus behind them, poured forth all his military learning, and concluded by invoking the name
of Vauban. Thurot was overruled, and Belfast was
saved by misplaced theories and eloquence, which
converted the half-dismantled castle of Carrickfergus
into very serviceable fortifications.[1]

The few raw recruits who formed the garrison of
Carrickfergus were diligently drilling when the enemy
landed 600 men, but directly the danger was known
they did what they could to put the castle in a state
of defence. The civic authorities did all in their
power to help the military. The Mayor quickly got
the militia under arms, sent forty of his " stout lads "
to Belfast with the French prisoners who had been
confined at Carrickfergus, and when invited to take
refuge in the castle bravely refused, saying " he would
go out with his dear boys and meet the poltroons and
have a knock at them." The worthy man was as good
as his word ; he placed his lads behind hedges and killed
forty-three of the enemy, including the commander.
The castle garrison was able to make a very poor
defence owing to lack of ammunition, but secured
good terms of capitulation.

When the news of the fall of Carrickfergus reached
Belfast every man who was able to carry a gun flew to
arms. The Roman Catholics offered to fight the
common enemy, and begged to be trusted with weapons.

---

[1] " Memoirs of James, Earl of Charlemont," p. 56.

One priest offered his own horse and daily pay to any young Protestant lad who would march down to Carrickfergus ; and several of the Protestant clergy marched out at the head of their congregations.[1] The peasantry from the surrounding districts thronged to the defence of Belfast. Lord Charlemont was much struck by the formidable appearance of his own tenants :

"They were drawn up in regular bodies, each with its chosen officers, and formed in martial array, some few with old firelocks, but the greater number armed with what is called in Scotland the Loughholer axe, a scythe longitudinally fixed to the end of a long pole, a desperate weapon."

It said much for Irish loyalty and self-control that though thousands were assembled in a small circuit the town was not disturbed by riots, brawls, or even drunkenness.[2] Contemporary evidence supports the view that if a raid had been made on the South Coast equal efforts would have been made to repel it.

By the time the news of the attack on Carrickfergus reached Dublin the three French frigates had become a formidable fleet, and Thurot's weather-beaten soldiers, in reality a ragged crew of pressed men and reprieved prisoners, were dignified by the title of veterans and multiplied by ten.[3] Bedford at once sent relief to Belfast, and directed Captain Elliot, who was stationed at Kinsale, to attack the French ships in Carrickfergus harbour. On February 26 Captain Ellot arrived off Carrickfergus with three ships of war, but was prevented by contrary winds from getting in. Thurot hastily embarked his men. Elliot gave chase and caught them on the 28th, between the Mull of Galway and the Isle of Man. The engagements lasted for an hour and a half, when all three French ships struck their colours. M. Thurot was among the killed, and his

---

[1] "Memoirs of James, Earl of Charlemont," p. 58.
[2] *Ibid.*
[3] Durand's "Memoirs of Thurot."

ship was so disabled that it nearly sank before it was got into Ramsay Bay. The French prisoners were taken to Belfast and made tolerably comfortable. They resigned themselves to their fate philosophically, and declared that any life on land was preferable to their late experience of " busking about the North seas for six months." [1] In March the City of Cork presented her freedom to Mr. Secretary Pitt, Admiral Hawke, and Captain Elliot as an expression of gratitude for their great and eminent services. Later in the year the Lord Lieutenant was able to return to England, and receive warm thanks and congratulations both from George II and Pitt upon the very satisfactory conclusion of his arduous task.

The efforts that Ireland made to raise forces for the Imperial war give some general idea of her resources. More direct evidence as to the economic condition of the country is supplied by a consideration of the use that Pitt made of Irish provisions both to victual his ships abroad and feed his citizens at home. In 1756 an embargo was laid on the exportation of provisions from the British Isles. [2] The loss of her foreign trade would soon have ruined Ireland if she had not found a profitable market for the goods by supplying the British Navy. Pitt granted numerous licences for ships laden with beef, pork, butter, and cheese to sail from Dublin and Cork to His Majesty's fleet stationed in the West Indies. He also allowed 64,000 pounds of beef to be sent to the royal magazines at Lisbon. [3] Sometimes Pitt was deceived ; it was not always possible to arrange for the Irish ships to sail under convoy, and several cargoes of good Irish beef went to cheer the hearts of the soldiers of the King of France. [4]

---

[1] S.P., Ireland, Colonel Sandford to Mr. Rigby, March 4, 1760.
[2] S.P., Ireland, Entry Books, 12, f. 135, Pitt to the Duke of Devonshire, Dec. 4, 1756.
[3] *Ibid.*, Pitt to Bedford, Jan. 4, 1757.
[4] S.P., Ireland, 417 ; and Woburn MSS. 67.

In 1757 there was a general scarcity of corn and provisions, and in self-preservation the British Parliament passed a series of Acts which incidentally gave great encouragement to Irish commerce. The importation of salted beef, pork, and butter from Ireland was allowed into England for six months, June to December, 1758, a duty of 1s. 3d. a cwt. being charged on beef and pork and 4d. a cwt. on salted butter. The preamble of this Act declared it to be for the benefit of both kingdoms, and this proved to be the case. It was renewed in 1758 and 1759, the duty being raised to 3s. 4d. a barrel for salted beef, pork, or butter, and 1s. 3d. per cwt. for dried beef tongues or dried hog's meat, " in order to be adequate to the duty payable for such quantity of salt as is requisite in curing or salting thereof." [1] After the accession of George III a law was passed nearly every year to allow the importation of Irish provisions until these temporary expedients gave place to a settled policy. [2]

There is no reason to believe that any of the measures of Pitt's first ministry from which Ireland benefitted were designed for the advantage of that kingdom. The embargo licences were usually obtained by London contractors, who probably profited more from them than the Irish merchants with whom they dealt. [3] The importation of Irish provisions into England was a measure passed to satisfy an English appetite rather than Irish grievance. In his Irish as in his American policy Pitt accepted the orthodox colonial theories of his day, but interpreted them according to his own generous nature. He sincerely believed that the Protestant colonists in Ireland had a duty to pay to the mother country, but he also saw that they had rights. They had a parliament, and to Pitt

---

[1] 31 George II, c. 28, and 33 George II, c. 5.
[2] Newenham, " View of Ireland," p. 160.
[3] " Account of Ireland, 1773," by Macartney, late Chief Secretary of the Kingdom.

the right of self-government was a sacred thing. Those who fought for the constitutional rights of Protestants in Ireland had his warmest support, and officials who neglected or exceeded their duty received justice untempered by mercy. For the Roman Catholic majority groaning under the iniquitous penal laws Pitt had no more pity than he had for the African slave. Politically he regarded Roman Catholicism as a menace to the Hanoverian dynasty; and as a form of the Christian faith Pitt had little sympathy with the doctrines of the Church of Rome. He himself defined the essence of religion as " a heart void of offence towards God and man; not subtle speculative opinions, but an active vital principle of faith." His advice to a young nephew in his first term at Cambridge was :

" Cherish true religion as preciously as you will fly with abhorrence and contempt superstition and enthusiasm. The first is the perfection and glory of the human nature; the two last the deprivation and disgrace of it." [1]

Macaulay has accused Pitt of being one of the few great characters who lacked simplicity. It is true that on public occasions he met the artificiality of his age with an extravagance which shocked it into genuine astonishment; but his inner life was marked by the simplicity of a recluse. None but a few real friends shared the happiness of his home. His most trusted colleagues were not allowed to surprise him in the study. Such a man has little sympathy with a form of religion which seems to him to place a priest between a man's conscience and his God.

His dealings with Ireland as Secretary of State taught Pitt that Irishmen were poor, but not devoid of enterprise, factious yet loyal. He saw that Ireland had wrongs, and determined to attempt cautious redress. In 1761 he refused to allow his own

---

[1] Chat. Corr., vol. i., pp. 70-76.

pension to be charged on the Irish list. In 1764 he gave Henry Flood a long audience at Hayes, and both then and afterwards warmly supported him in his scheme for an Irish militia. One of the first measures of Chatham's ill-fated administration was to provide that the Lord Lieutenant should reside continuously in Ireland.[1] The independence of the judges, a militia Bill, a Habeas Corpus Act, and the limitation of the duration of Parliament were the chief Irish measures discussed at Chatham's first cabinets.[2] Had his health not broken down the course of history might have been changed, for who shall say that in 1766 the Irish problem was not capable of solution by a minister who described Ireland as a country " whose welfare every thinking Englishman will ever consider as his own " ? [3]

---

[1] " Life of Lord Macartney," vol. i., p. 38.
[2] S.P., Ireland, 425, Shelburne to Townshend, Oct. 29, 1767.
[3] Chat. Corr., vol. iii., p. 4, Chatham to Henry Flood, March 15, 1766.

CHAPTER VII

INDIA

" Trade is an extended and complicated consideration : it reaches as far as ships can sail or winds can blow : it is a great and various machine. To regulate the numberless movements of its several parts, and combine them into effect, for the good of the whole, requires the superintending wisdom and energy of the supreme power of the empire."—Chatham, Speech on January 20, 1775.

PITT's views with regard to the empire acquired in India during his ministry have long been a source of fruitful conjecture. Most of his biographers begin Chatham's Life with a synopsis of that of his grandfather, the irascible old Governor of Madras, whose famous diamond was the foundation stone of the fortunes of the Pitt family. But there is no evidence that Governor Pitt gave his grandson a more illuminating account of his early experiences than testy old men usually vouchsafe to the " hopeful lad " among their descendants. The Pitt family were not communicative or united. Chatham had to seek out his own path in life. No friendly guide told him of those signposts which he so carefully pointed out to his own son and nephew. His childhood was unhappy and his education unsuitable. All his best possessions came to him late in life as rewards for which he had consciously striven. It may be that the shrewd intellect of the old Nabob was transmitted to his grandson. It is possible that knowledge acquired in one may survive a second or third generation. But as yet we know little of these things. They are beyond the ken of the historian. History shows us a man as seen by his contemporaries and judged by posterity. It leaves him his own soul and allows his ancestors to rest in peace.

It was not till he became Secretary of State that Pitt was confronted with his first Indian problem. On December 21, 1756, the Secret Committee of the East India Company sent him a detailed account of their annual expenses, pointing out the increase of their liabilities " during the periods of the French embroils," and begging for financial and military assistance.[1] Pitt considered the matter carefully. As usual, when confronted with something outside his previous political experience, he took every step to become acquainted with the essentials of the matter in hand. On Christmas Day he put the subject before his colleagues in the Cabinet.[2] On Sunday, January 3, he had a long conversation with Mr. Payne, the chairman of the Secret Committee,[3] and on January 9 he wrote to the Company directing them to send him detailed accounts of the plans they had formed for the conduct of the last and the present war.[4] A consideration of these gave the Secretary of State reason to hope that the Company had " a perfect knowledge of their own affairs." This supposition formed the sound basis of Pitt's Indian policy. The plan which the directors submitted to him was threefold. It included a scheme of alliance with native powers, an attack on Pondicherry, and the reduction of the Island of Mauritius.[5] The object of the East India Company was purely commercial, but no eighteenth-century merchant could be unaware of the great truth that trade rests upon the sword. The directors had no desire to risk their revenue in fortifications, and were

---

[1] India Office Home Miscellaneous 94.
[2] Basil Williams, " Pitt," vol. i., p. 300.
[3] India Office Home Miscellaneous 94, Jan. 5, 1757.
[4] Chatham MSS. 99.
[5] *Ibid.*, Secret Committee of the East India Company to Pitt, Jan. 12, 1757.

loth to expend their energies in the administration
of an empire, but they knew that the naval station
at Mauritius was the root of French commercial
power, Pondicherry the main stem, and Chandernagore
a fruitful branch.[1]   Once convinced of the soundness
of their schemes, Pitt did all in his power to aid the
Company.   He sent them men, ships, and money ;
and enhanced the gift a thousandfold by the manner
of the giving.   For he strengthened the Company
by support where a lesser man might have weakened
them by patronage.   Colonel Aldercron, who was in
command of His Majesty's forces in India when Pitt
succeeded to office, had failed to co-operate amicably
with the Company's officers.   He was promptly
recalled, and directed to encourage his men to enter
the Company's service.   Draper, who was sent to
replace him, was a picked man and a personal friend
of Pitt's.[2]   He and his troops were placed in a position
of financial dependence upon the East India Company,
who paid them the difference between their scale
of pay and that of the Government.   It is noteworthy
that Parliament refunded this money as part of their
annual grant to the Company.   The correspondence
that passed between Draper and the Secret Committee
is characteristic of the care that Pitt's officers bestowed
upon the economic welfare of their men.   The future
gallant conqueror of Manilla requested that he might
be informed as to the exact allowances his men would
receive, that he might explain it to the regiment for
their encouragement.   He petitioned that a few sober
women might be allowed to accompany the troops
for washing and other uses, and fraternally desired
that the captains of the ships on which the regiment

----

[1] " Selections from Records of the Government of India, 1748-
1767," vol. i., p. 91, J. Long.
[2] Chat. MSS. 31.   *Cf.* Walter Frewen Lord, " The Lost Possessions
of England for Draper and the Manilla Expedition."

was embarked would prevent their sailors from gaming with the soldiers for their necessaries.

Five years later Draper described this regiment as " real veterans," " my tenth indeed my only legion." With their aid he captured Manilla against overwhelming odds, and their moderation in the hour of victory was the supreme test of the mettle of the 79th.[1]

But though Pitt did what he could to strengthen the land forces of the Company, it was with his fleet that he hoped they would strike the decisive blow. On Jan. 11, 1757, he wrote to Admiral Watson, directing him to help the Company in the execution of any plans they might form for distressing the enemy. The plan which Pitt had in his mind was an attack upon Mauritius, but he knew the feasibility of this could be better judged at Madras. Nor did he forget that the Eastern Squadron had its own special work of commerce protection. His orders to the Admirals concerning co-operation with the Company's servants were always conditional.[2]

For Clive's victories at Calcutta, Chandernagore, and Plassey Pitt had neither responsibility nor credit. But they served to justify his opinion that the Company's " heaven-born general " was the best judge of their affairs. Although " not born for a desk," Clive was well grounded in the value of economic strategy ; he gave it as his opinion that the capture of Chandernagore (the granary of the islands) was of more consequence to the Company than the taking of Pondicherry itself, and declared that if the Nabob could be induced to give up the French factories " this will be driving them out root and branch. I am well informed, without Chandernagore the islands must

---

[1] C.O. 77, 20.
[2] J. S. Corbett, " England in the Seven Years' War," vol. i., p. 336.

starve, and Pondicherry suffer greatly." [1] Clive's predictions were verified four years later, when news came home from Madras that Pondicherry had been " reduced rather by famine than force." [2]

In one of his most closely reasoned speeches, Chatham described oversea trade as a great and various machine which required the superintending wisdom and energy of the supreme power of the empire. During the seven years' war Pitt was supreme, and the substantial help he sent to the East India Company supplied that great machine with the form of energy it needed most. But the Secretary of State's labours did not end with letters to the Admiralty and Ordnance board ; he neglected no opportunity of adding to the wisdom of his superintending power. The Court of Directors kept him well supplied with accurate information, and the Secretary of State was careful to discover exactly what value the good merchants of London attached to the various successes and reverses of their arms in the East.[3] In 1758 Clive sent Pitt a detailed account of the revenues of Bengal.

On November 20, 1759, Clive's Secretary, Walsh, had a long interview with Pitt, and delivered him the famous letter in which Clive tried to tempt the Secretary of State to make the Government an active partner in the administration of the great empire of Eastern trade.[4] But Pitt was not to be drawn from his first position. He had not yet decided into which channel he should divert the stream of gold controlled by the machine under his hand. " He said the Company were not proper to have it, nor the crown, for such a revenue would endanger our liberties," and

---

[1] " Bengalia, 1756-1757 " (Indian Record Series), S. C. Hill, vol. ii., p. 310. Extracts from a letter from Colonel Clive to Mr. Pigot, March 29, 1757.
[2] I.O. Miscellaneous Letters Received, 43. Robert Nairne to Cl. Barrow, Esq., Madras, Jan. 25, 1761.
[3] I.O. Miscellaneous Letters Received, 42, Whitehall, Dec. 3, 1760.
[4] Malcolm's " Life of Clive," vol. ii., p. 128.

declared that Clive had shown his good sense " by the application of it to the public." Pitt's last words suggest a wise and liberal policy, but one far in advance of his age. The Indian trade could only be secured by the united action of the members of a strong corporation. The Government or the Company seemed the only possible alternatives, yet there were grave reasons against giving the control of so great a revenue to either. In 1759 Pitt had found no solution to this problem. But with him suspended judgment did not necessitate vacillating measures. The harvest must be reaped, though it were uncertain who should garner it. He asked Walsh about Mauritius ; " whether the reduction of that would not be laying the axe to the root, and how far it was practicable." As a parting benediction, Pitt threw out a hint that the Government intended to assist the Company with four men-of-war and 1,000 men. Three days later the Secret Committee of the East India Company sent a very important despatch to the Presidencies of Bombay and Madras. In these documents Clive's letter was quoted and Pitt's suggestions applied. The Secret Committee declared that the distress to which the French had been reduced both in Europe and Asia had encouraged them to form definite plans for the siege of Pondicherry, which, if successful, was to be followed by an attack upon the French islands.[1] A year later Pitt wrote strongly to Admiral Stevens, reminding him of the general directions given to Watson in 1757, and, that there might be no possibility of mistake, expressly commanding him to co-operate with the servants of the Company should they see fit to make an attack upon Mauritius.[2]

---

[1] C.O. 77, 20. Extract from a letter from the Secret Committee of the East India Company to the Select Committee at Fort St. George, Nov. 23, 1759.
[2] Chat. MSS, 100.

Admiral Stevens died on May 20, 1761, and the command of the English squadron in the East devolved upon Rear-Admiral Cornish, who then for the first time was made aware of the long-intended expedition which the fall of Pondicherry had at last made practicable. His annoyance was great at finding that though the design had been suggested to the Presidencies in despatches dated November 23, 1759, they had not given Admiral Stevens notice of their plans till March 21, 1761. There had been good reason for secrecy. In 1759 the Secret Committee had concluded their letter to the Select Committee at Bombay with a solemn warning: "These are our sentiments and intentions,we conjure you to keep them most inviolably secret ; the time we hope is certainly near at hand to carry them into execution, but once known all future attempts may be frustrated." The Presidency of Fort St. George were also cautioned: "If circumstances should not admit of your carrying any part of this one plan into execution, you are nevertheless strictly enjoined to as strict secrecy, because we have reason to hope the time is not very distant for our taking it up again." [1]

With Pitt also the Mauritius expedition was a fixed idea. The opportunity only had been wanting. In January, 1761, he thought he saw his way to send the necessary forces, and sent news to Admiral Stevens that an expedition was being sent out under Commodore Keppel. The instructions reached Cornish at Bombay in July. He joyfully sent word to Madras that he was concerned with the King's Service, and sailed away for the rendezvous, where he waited in vain ; for at the last moment Keppel's expedition had been diverted to Belleisle.[2] It is significant that

---

[1] C.O. 77, 20.
[2] For the Mauritius Expedition, see J. S. Corbett, " England in the Seven Years' War."

on the only occasion when Pitt departed from this general rule, and acted independently of the East India Company, grave confusion resulted. If Cornish had not received news of plans formed in England, he would have done all in his power to carry out those which were being made on the spot, for though he criticised these severely, he admitted that where so much was to be gained, " the entire ruin of the French commerce in India," something might be left to chance.[1]

But if Pitt must bear the blame for the miscarriage of the expedition to Mauritius, he should be given his fair share of the glory of the capture of Manilla. For though this plan was not seriously entertained by the ministry till after Pitt's resignation, his contribution to its success was no small one. It was carried out by veterans trained in his wars, led by officers whom he had encouraged " not to stay to careen this or condemn that," but " whose presence of mind astonished the Indies."[2]   The capture of Manilla was due not to the minister who authorised the expedition, but to the heroes who executed it. It was described by its leader as a *coup de main*. On the eve of the attack, Draper declared his hopes of success were founded upon the following reasons: " We have unanimity for our Base, which I build much upon, and the Zeal and Ardour of Mr. Cornish and all the Gentlemen of the Navy who have promised to assist me to the utmost with the seamen and marines, and I do not doubt but their spirit and activity will make ample amends for any Want of Regularity."[3]

Pitt vigorously defended Draper against the charges that were brought against him in later days by Spain, and declared him to be " a Gallant conqueror . . .

---

[1] C.O. 77, 20.
[2] Chat. Corr., vol. i., p. 341, note.
[3] C.O. 77, 20, Draper to Egremont, July 27, 1762. See Appendix.

whose noble and generous spirit would do honour to the noblest grandee." The general's own account of the expedition, written in the first flush of victory, bears out Pitt's view of the writer. He makes light of his own share in the action, rejoices that he has been able " to save so fine a city from destruction," and speaks little of the monetary value of his conquest, except to justify the ransom : " Considering their Critical Situation and vast Opulence, the terms were as Reasonable for them as Beneficial to us." His brother officers are given a generous share of credit for the success, and the tribute he pays his soldiers should live as a memorial to those noble men of private rank who died at our Empire's birth.

" It is with particular satisfaction that I can assure your Lordship that the Firm Bravery and Perseverance of the troops could only be equalled by their Humanity after Victory ; notwithstanding the great Provocations given them to enforce all the Rigour and Severities of War ; As my Secretary Lieutenant Fryar had been murdered with a flag of truce in his Hand ; but our People remembered their National Character more than Vengeance, or the Punishment due to the Enemy : they received all the supplications for mercy.

.   .   .   .   .

" In the last Place may I presume to point out the Services of the 79th Regiment, which, upon the good conduct of their Former and Present Field Officers, has the Peculiar Merit of having First stopt the Progress of the French in India : and not a little contributed to the Happy turn and Decision of that War under Colonel Coote ; and has since Conquered in the Utmost Verge of Asia. 23 officers with upwards of 800 men have fallen in the Cause of their Country since the Regiment left England. Numbers of the Survivors are wounded. Your Lordships Goodness encourages me to Mention them as Objects of Compassion and Protection." [1]

But small use was there in appealing to the compassion of the ministry that ruthlessly signed away the conquests bought with better men's blood. When Draper returned home he had the humiliation of finding his magnificent work belittled and his generous offers of further service contemptuously put aside. Perhaps he found some consolation in composing the inscription for the triumphal arch which he erected in his garden to the memory of William Pitt. [2]

But when all that is known of Pitt's dealings with India is told, the great problem remains : What were Chatham's matured views of that Empire which, of all the glorious possessions acquired during his administration, lay nearest his heart ? [3] What were his plans for the future of a dominion which he declared was to be preferred even to America ? In 1757 Pitt granted the East India Company the right to retain the spoils of victory. In 1759 he politely waved aside Clive's suggestion that the Government should appropriate the revenues of the Company's conquests. Pitt feared wealth as much as he desired it ; and was quick to see that a wise distribution of the riches of the East might prove a more difficult task than that of acquiring them. Corruption was the most sinister factor in eighteenth-century politics. In 1770

---

[1] C.O. 77, 20, Draper to Egremont, Manilla, Nov. 2, 1762.
[2] " Qui orbem fere universum animo complexus
    Hostibus terra mariq. profligatis
  Europam Asiam Africam Americam
      Victoriis Peragavit
      Triumphis illustravit."
Chat. Corr., vol. iii., p. 326.
[3] " America sits heavy upon my mind. India is a perpetual source of regrets. There ' where I had garnered up my heart '; where our strength lay, and our happiest resources presented themselves, it is all changed into danger, weakness, distraction and vulnerability."—Chat. Corr., vol. iv., p. 331. The Earl of Chatham to the Earl of Shelburne, Burton Pynsent, March 6, 1774.

Chatham had good reason to declare that for some years past there had been an influx of wealth into the country, which had been attended with many fatal consequences because it had not been the regular and natural produce of labour and industry.[1] Three years later wrongs suffered in the East distracted his attention from the evildoers of the West, and while praising the efforts made by the East India Company to put their house in order, Chatham urged upon the Ministry the duty of intervention on behalf of the native races.

"The abolition of inland trade on private account is highly laudable, as far as that provision goes ; but I would assuredly carry the prohibition further, and open again to the natives and other eastern merchants the inland trade of Bengal, and abolish all monopolies on the Company's account ; which now operate to the unjust exclusion of an oppressed people, and to the impoverishing and alienating of those extensive and populous provinces. The hearts and good affections of Bengal are of more worth than all the profits of ruinous and odious monopolies."

Such words recall those in which Chatham declared that America was too great an object to be grasped but in the arms of affection. In the East as in the West, Pitt's period of power was also one of probation ; and while faithfully administering the things of the old order he had a vision of the new.

---

[1] "Almon," vol. ii., p. 212.   Speech on the State of the Nation, 1770.

CHAPTER VIII

THE SECRETARY OF STATE FOR THE SOUTHERN DEPARTMENT

PART I

THE ECONOMIC IMPLICATIONS IN THE POLICY PURSUED
BY PITT AS SECRETARY OF STATE FOR THE SOUTHERN
DEPARTMENT

"To outlast our enemy was worth perseverance."—Pitt, May 12,
1763.

As Secretary of State for the Southern Department,
Pitt controlled the correspondence between Great
Britain and France, Spain, Portugal, Italy, Turkey, and
the Barbary States. He also exercised a certain supervision over that which his colleague Holdernesse
carried on with the Northern capitals. Pitt's letters
to British ambassadors and consuls in Southern Europe
deal primarily with political matters. His correspondents were instructed to endeavour to frustrate
the union of France and Spain; to strengthen the
Anglo-Portuguese alliance; to stir up the distrust
with which the courts of Madrid, Naples, and Turin
viewed the designs of Austria upon Italy; to persuade the Grand Seigneur to aid our Prussian ally by
an attack on Hungary. None of these questions were
without economic implications. The Family Compact included a commercial treaty.[1] The Anglo-
Portuguese alliance was threatened by a war of Tariffs.[2]

---

[1] Chat. MSS. 88, Mackenzie to Pitt, Turin, Jan. 30, 1760.
[2] S.P.F., Portugal, 52, 53.

Pitt used economic arguments in his endeavour to detach the courts of Naples and Madrid from their union with Versailles and Vienna ; [1] and seized upon a dearth in the Ottoman Empire to try to persuade the Porte that salvation lay in a Prussian alliance.[2] But quite apart from the incidental connection which must always exist between political and economic questions, a commercial principle ruled Pitt's statecraft. His great object was to enable Great Britain to outlast France without undue exhaustion. His conquests were designed to pay for the war, and he knew that while success was uniform adequate supplies would be forthcoming. Union of measures was essential for such a policy. America was won in Germany, because it cost less to transport troops to Minden than Quebec ; the destruction of French commerce in the Levant prevented supplies from being sent to the West Indies ; and British cruisers in the Mediterranean protected the colonial fish trade with Spain, Portugal, and the Italian States. All privateering questions belonged to the Secretary of State's department rather than the Admiralty, and privateering was essentially an economic method of warfare.

For the purpose of the present study, these aspects of the Great Commoner's European policy which have colonial and commercial implications have been given a prominence which perhaps they hardly deserve. They were an integral part of his design, a necessary background which was never allowed to detract the master's eye from the chief features of his composition. Nothing was too small for Pitt's statecraft, no interest sufficiently powerful to escape his control. A villainous privateer captain who cheated his creditors, " carted his children round Europe to arouse com-

---

[1] S.P.F., Sicily and Naples, 15, Pitt to Sir James Gray, Sept. 16, 1757.
[2] S.P.F., Turkey, 40, Pitt to Porter, March 2, 1758 ; May 25, 1759.

passion," and took refuge behind the Venetian laws of inheritance, was pursued by the righteous indignation of the Secretary of State;[1] but when the interests of the merchants trading to Portugal threatened to bring about a breach with His Most Faithful Majesty, Pitt could turn a deaf ear to a just complaint. Nor were the grievances of an English mining company in Sardinia allowed to disturb the neutrality of a power so delicately poised between the territories of Vienna and Versailles.[2] Pitt was playing an intricate game. Sometimes his pieces got into strange places. Part of the expedition which he sent to capture Goree was wrecked on the coast of Morocco, and the survivors had to be rescued from the terrible fate of Moorish slavery by the Secretary of State for the Southern Department.

A barrel of sugar captured by a British privateer in the Atlantic found its way through the course of trade to Rome, and on being opened by a merchant there was discovered to contain papers which proved that Dutch officials were covering French trade in the West Indies.[3]

Accidents and incidents must not be confused with fundamentals. From an economic point of view, the chief value of the Secretary of State's European correspondence lay in the information he thus gained as to the financial condition of his enemies.[4] After Hawke's victory over Conflans, Pitt knew that the French marine was ruined, and that the country had neither men nor money to fit another fleet. But when blamed for continuing the expense of a great marine after that victory his defence was unassailable.

---

[1] S.P.F., Venice, 67, Pitt to Murray, Whitehall, Nov. 29, 1757.
[2] S.P.F., Savoy and Sardinia, 65, 66, 67. Various letters. Cf. 66, Pitt to Bristol, March 21, 1758; Wood to Mackenzie, 67, March 16, 1759.
[3] S.P.F., Tuscany, 66, Florence, Aug. 18, 1759, Mann to Pitt.
[4] The correspondence between Mackenzie and Pitt, S.P.F., Savoy and Sardinia, 67, is specially valuable for this.

" Spain was in a common cause with France,—the Swedes, the Genoese, and even the Dutch were ready to lend their ships for hire." [1] All this the Secretary of State learned through his European correspondence.[2] His measures were framed on these calculations. After 1760, Pitt knew that Great Britain and her allies were a match for any possible combination of powers France could array against her, but he took no risks. It was worth while to pay for a Mediterranean squadron in order to keep open the ports of Sardinia and Portugal, Naples, Genoa, and Venice. Nor must it be forgotten that it was through their trade with these ports that the American colonies gained the specie which enabled them to make their returns to Great Britain,[3] the 2,000,000 a year which Pitt afterwards declared had carried Great Britain triumphantly through the war.

Judged on their own merits, three commercial questions with which the Secretary of State for the Southern Department had to deal have a certain interest. Pitt's first ministry coincided with a crisis in our commercial relations with Portugal. His dealings with the Barbary States were almost entirely concerned with slavery or human merchandise. The privateering question needed as careful manipulation in the Mediterranean as across the Atlantic, and intimately concerned illicit trade carried on by British subjects and those of the Ottoman Empire and Italian States.

---

[1] Pitt's Speech on the Preliminaries for Peace, Dec. 9, 1762.
[2] Cf. G. L. Beer, " British Colonial Policy."
[3] Speech on the Preliminaries.

CHAPTER IX

THE SECRETARY OF STATE FOR THE SOUTHERN DEPARTMENT

PART II

PORTUGAL

" Portugal is in the immediate predicament of nearness to us after Ireland and our colonies. It assists without draining us."

    •   ᴗ   •   •   •   •

" If you as a maritime power cannot protect Portugal, Genoa will next be shut against you and then the ports of Sardinia—what ports shut against the first maritime power in the world ! "—Pitt's Speech on Supplies voted for Portugal.

PITT's first ministry coincided with a crisis in Anglo-Portuguese commercial relations. With the accession of Joseph I, in 1750, Sebastian de Carvalhoe Mello, better known by his later title of Marquis of Pombal, had become chief minister of the most autocratic power in Europe. His policy was national, but not democratic ; he desired to see a prosperous, contented Portugal smilingly obeying the wise behests of her master. Three obstacles stood between him and his ideal—the pride of nobles, the guile of Jesuits, and the astute intelligence of English traders. England, he declared, had conquered Portugal without the expense of warfare. Everywhere Portuguese trade passed through English hands, and the balance was always in favour of Great Britain. To remedy this, in 1755 he revived an old statute forbidding the extraction of bullion, and in 1756 founded joint stock companies to conduct the wine trade and the trade with Brazil. British merchants complained loudly both of the infringement of treaties granting freedom of commerce and of particular hardships in the working of the new regulations.[1] The Consul-General at Lisbon sent Pitt detailed accounts of the merchants' grievances. The question was one of great difficulty. Portugal had an undoubted right to regulate her own commerce, but she had so few industries that trade with Great Britain could not be carried on without the extraction of bullion. Also it appeared very hard to the English factory at Oporto that they could no longer carry on a trade to which they had a prescriptive right without investing their capital in a company in whose conduct they would have no voice unless they became naturalised subjects of Portugal. The Secretary of State was inundated with petitions from merchants engaged in the Portugal trade, and spent many nights in considering them, but though his Portuguese policy was influenced by economic considerations its main object was political. While he watched the union between France and Spain becoming closer, his determination that nothing should be allowed to interrupt the good understanding between England and Portugal grew stronger. In 1760 he sent Lord Kinnoul as a special ambassador to the court of Lisbon to apologise for the infraction of the laws of nations committed by the capture of French ships under the guns of the fort of Lagos. The real object of Kinnoul's mission was to combat French and Spanish influence, but he was instructed to use economic arguments, and to point out that Portugal had little to gain or fear from France, " that haughty but impotent court." The ambassador was also directed to try to obtain satisfaction for the merchants, but not to delay his departure on that account after the first object of his mission had been attained.

---

[1] *Cf.* Shillington and Chapman, " Commercial Relations between England and Portugal."

In this Kinnoul was completely successful. Pombal admitted that France was powerless. " Their marine destroyed, their commerce ruined, their population diminished, their agriculture neglected, their finances so exhausted that they do not know how to find the means of supplying the necessary expenses of the war."[1] The removal of the fear that Portugal might join France and Spain was a great point gained. Pitt's object was to outlast the enemy. In 1760 he knew that the resources of France were almost exhausted, but he had one thing to fear, and that was a union of the maritime powers of Europe. His foreign correspondents all told him the same tale. Holland, Denmark, Sweden, and the Italian States were all covering French trade.[2] It was no time to attempt to dictate to Portugal as to the regulations by which she should control her industries and commerce. Pitt was waging war on a large scale for and upon trade ; it was part of his policy to keep open the ports of Portugal, but this did not satisfy the English merchants trading to that country. One whom the consul at Lisbon described as " James Groset, a merchant in London of a restless turbulent disposition,"[3] sent threatening letters to the Secretary of State's office, declaring that the merchants trading to Portugal were like snails who had been trampled on long enough, and that if they did not obtain redress or the assurance of it, they would put out their horns, lay the facts of the case before the Lord Mayor, publish an account of their grievances all over the nation, and bring the question before the Bar of the House.[4]

But Pitt was already on the horns of a dilemma, when he was accused in the House of having neglected the

---

[1] Kinnoul to Pitt, April 16, 1760, quoted in " Memoirs of the Marquis of Pombal," by John Smith, 1843.

[2] S.P.F., Savoy and Sardinia, 65 and 66.

[3] S.P.F., Portugal, 54, Frankland to Wood, Lisbon, Jan. 24, 1761.

[4] Ibid., 53, Grosett to Wood, Nov. 29, 1760.

complaints of Portuguese merchants. " He insisted
that, so far from it, he had spent many nights in considering them, and referred that gentleman to what
had passed between him and the ambassador of the
court of Portugal." These papers completely vindicate the Secretary of State from a charge of neglect
or indifference.[1] Pitt was well aware of the value of
our trade with Portugal, and the danger of the new
encroachments upon it ; but he also realised that
Pombal, for whom he had a sincere admiration, was
doing very much what he himself would have done
in his place. Pitt regarded Portugal not as an enemy
to be trampled underfoot, nor yet as an infant state
to be carried where its protector willed, but as an
ally to be courted and helped. He gave the minutest
care and consideration to all sides of the Portuguese
question until he was forced to relinquish office, and
then he advised his successors :

" We must set Portugal on his legs, not take him on
our shoulders."

---

[1] See Appendix.

CHAPTER X

THE SECRETARY OF STATE FOR THE SOUTHERN DEPARTMENT

PART III

THE BARBARY STATES

" If the merchant in the Indies and America is proud and haughty, in Africa he is submissive and cringing. He pays and very dearly for the right of purchasing the productions of that rich but too much neglected country."—From " Travels through Barbary," by Abbé Poiret, 1755.

In the eighteenth century the relations between Great Britain and the Barbary States were almost wholly economic and peculiarly in need of export supervision.[1] The self-styled Emperor of Morocco and the Turkish generals who ruled over Algiers, Tunis, and Tripoli openly engaged in the profession of piracy, and carried on a highly lucrative traffic in Christian slaves. Their cruisers preyed upon the merchant ships of every nation who could not secure a treaty of peace and commerce with their masters, and such a treaty was only to be gained by yearly payments which placed the great powers of Europe in the position of tributary states. Great Britain compromised by presenting gifts on the occasion of the appointment of a consul instead of paying an annual sum. The distinction was only a nominal one ; " it was well understood that the consular presents were the price of the Mediterranean passes,

---

[1] *Cf.* Playfair, " The Scourge of Christendom " ; Lane-Poole, " The Barbary Corsairs."

which secured British merchantmen immunity from the attacks of Barbary Corsairs. This system encouraged Barbary rulers to make their consul's position unbearable, and so to secure frequent relays of envoys and gifts." An eighteenth-century Dey was the personification of " the economic man." Self-interest was his ruling passion. Of necessity fearless and temperate, he usually owed his position to a successful revolt, and kept it only so long as his mind was sufficiently alert to detect the plots that were always maturing in the brains of his ambitious followers. His physical fitness and powers of endurance made the Moor a coveted slave, but in a ruler these virtues were counterbalanced by inhuman cruelty and absolute disregard for the obligations of truth and justice. There were in fact but two ways of dealing with a North African potentate ; you must either convince him that it was to his advantage to be your ally, or that he would suffer materially by your enmity. The position was simple ; here was no question of family compact or traditional alliance, balance of power or wars of religion.

Pitt's dealings with the Barbary States show how carefully he studied the question of their commercial relations with Great Britain, and afford another example of the way in which he only resorted to a show of force after he had failed to achieve his ends by peaceful methods. In 1757 Great Britain's relations with Morocco were strained almost to breaking point. The treaty made between the two kingdoms in 1751 had expired ; and a short truce which had been hurriedly patched up was drawing to a close. Should the Emperor of Morocco not be persuaded to renew the treaties, his cruisers would be let loose upon British commerce, and the garrison of Gibraltar and the British fleet in the Mediterranean would be deprived of a convenient source of fresh provisions.

In the spring of 1756 Mr. Whateley, an English

merchant residing at Marseilles, had been appointed British consul to Morocco; as, however, on the declaration of war with France he had been obliged to leave Marseilles and his whereabouts could not be ascertained, Pitt selected James Read, an English merchant who had spent some years at Gibraltar and taken an active and public-spirited part in the management of the factory, to be Consul-General for Great Britain at the court of Tetuan. By his instructions Read was directed to deliver the customary presents to the Prince Sedy Mahomet, and in addition was given £1,500 to employ for the release of British captives. He was also strongly advised to endeavour to avoid supplying the Emperor with the naval stores he always demanded, but which Pitt feared might give umbrage to the court of Spain.[1] Read's mission was a complete failure. The Prince, who had become Emperor by his father's death, refused to discuss a treaty with an envoy who brought letters from Mr. Secretary Pitt, and demanded a different ambassador with credentials from King George. An unlucky collision between a British cruiser and one of the Emperor's ships still further complicated matters. Read and his companion, Lieutenant Grosvenor, were summoned to appear before His Imperial Highness Sedy Mahomet, who, on their refusal to promise him a new cruiser, called them "rogues, rascals, and villains, said that the English were the worst of all nations, and that he wished the French or Spaniards were in the possession of Gibraltar that he might not have such bad neighbours." The Emperor then ordered the British envoys to be driven out of his presence and confined in a dungeon. Shortly afterwards he sent them a message that if they did not give him a draft on their government for 20,000 ducats before next morning he would burn them. Read complied with this demand, and they

---

[1] S.P.F., Barbary States, 20, Pitt to Read, Whitehall, July 26, 1757.

were released.   But two days later the consul was told
that he must go and work with the government slaves,
whereupon he locked himself into his room and blew
out his brains.   Sedy Mahomet sent for Lieutenant
Grosvenor, expressed his surprise at the tragedy, and
suggested that the late consul must either have been
out of his senses or drunk.[1]

The failure of Read's expedition opened Pitt's eyes
to the real state of affairs in Morocco.   He decided
henceforth to settle all disputes with that power
through the Governor of Gibraltar, and to back his
negociations with a show of naval force.[2]   This policy
was entirely successful.   Lord Home brought Sedy
Mahomet to terms on the three disputed questions
of the ransom of British slaves, the compensation
for the damaged cruiser, and the value of the consular
gifts.   Captain Milbanke then sailed for Sallée with
two men-of-war, a frigate and a boat vessel, embarked
the captives, paid the ransom, and then proceeded to
Fez, where, on July 28, 1760, he secured the Emperor's
signature to a treaty of peace and commerce.   Besides
confirming all the old treaties, this peace contained
an important new article, expressly permitting Great
Britain to buy flour and wheat for the garrisons of
Gibraltar and Minorca (when it should be restored),
and for the British fleet in the Mediterranean, from any
part of the dominions of the Emperor of Morocco.[3]
No one can retreat more gracefully from an untenable
situation than an Oriental despot.   The letter which
the Emperor of Morocco sent to George III with the
new commercial treaty is a study in diplomacy.   The
tyrant who had driven the merchant consul to be

---

[1] S.P.F., Barbary States, 20, f. 256.   Heads of a narrative humbly
offered to the Right Hon. Wm. Pitt, Esq., by Wm. Grosvenor, Lieut. in
H.M. Marine Forces.
[2] S.P.F., Various, 70, Pitt to Home, Feb. 6, 1700.
[3] S.P.F., Barbary States, 20, Milbanke to Pitt, Aug. 6, 1760.

his own executioner writes suavely of the naval officer whose cruisers lay in the Sallée roads :

" Your Ambassador Mark Milbanke, Esq., came to me, to whom I granted all his pleasure, and had much discourse with and found him to be a man of great sense and understanding more than any ambassador I ever had before, and for that reason I shewed him all the Honour and kindness possible, and as a proof I have a great esteem for him, I agreed to all the treaties which subsisted in the time of Muley Ismael of Glorious memory. The ambassador also asked me for your additional articles which I granted him, and there was nothing he required of me but I complied with and delivered to him all the English subjects, as also the passengers on board Portuguese ships and likewise two Minorquins Jaime and Pedro, who were people of great use to me, and had it not been for the sake of Your Britanic Majesty I would not have parted from them, and beg Your Majesty to take care of them and have them near your person as I had, as they'll be very necessary betwixt our two crowns, and they will be very proper in case I want anything from England or England from me to represent it betwixt us. If this Ambassador Mark Milbanke Esq., had been sent to me before, the peace had been settled long ago, he being a very proper man for the business and very agreeable and courteous in his Behaviour and Talking." [1]

In 1757 similar disputes were pending between Great Britain and Algiers. There were only two British merchants living in that state, but they contrived to embitter the life of their consul, and nearly brought about a rupture with the Algerines. Consul Aspinwall sent Pitt many complaints of the conduct of these men, whom he described as " half Algerines," and " downright Jackall's to these voracious Lyons."

---

[1] C.O. 389, 49.

He declared that " these two persons who call themselves merchants and are the only British ones in all
the Algerine Dominions, have no trade at all with
England ; their whole subsistence seems to depend
on the success of the Algerine cruisers, and buying
shares of their prizes, which I know not whether it
can be called Merchandize or rather a living upon
plunder." [1]

Their means of livelihood gave the merchants
interests in common with the Algerines, which were
directly opposed to those of the British consul. It
was to the advantage of Messrs. Cruize and Gibson
to secure the condemnation of prizes, since they
occasionally made 100 per cent. profit on the purchase
and sale of the cargoes. Before the appointment
of Mr. Aspinwall in 1754, Mr. Ford, a merchant of
Biddeford, had frequently acted as consul, and both the
Dey and the merchants were anxious to make Aspinwall's position untenable and secure the consulate
for Ford. Aspinwall was a just man, and Pitt supported him for four years, but finally, at his own
request, allowed him to return to England to mend
his damaged health and fortunes.

During Pitt's ministry the chief difficulties with
Algiers related to questions of trade and navigation.
As the Algerines carried on a considerable trade with
our enemies the French, and constantly preyed upon
the commerce of neutral Spain, very complicated
privateering cases often occurred. When Pitt took office
he succeeded to the entanglements of a dispute between
the Dey of Algiers, the King of Spain, Consul Aspinwall, and the merchant Cruize. In 1755 Cruize
had sent a ship to Tripoly to fetch a cargo of corn for
the Dey. The ship had been captured by a Spanish
cruiser, legally condemned, the crew imprisoned, and
the cargo sold. But on receiving assurance from

---

[1] S.P.F., Barbary States, 10, f. 274.

Great Britain that the ship belonged to an English merchant, the crew had been released and some compensation given for the cargo. Still the Dey, who had lost over the transaction, pressed Cruize for compensation, and when the merchant met his demands half-way, turned to the consul for the remainder of the sum. Aspinwall wrote to Pitt for directions, who replied that he had enquired into the matter thoroughly, and as there was sufficient evidence that Mr. Cruize had been covering the trade of the enemies of Spain with British colours, he must naturally bear the loss, which fact the Secretary of State hoped would deter other of His Majesty's subjects from engaging in a similar traffic.[1] The consul took this letter to the Dey, who coolly replied that it was a forgery. Aspinwall held out as long as he could, but finally, considering what a violent government he had to deal with, paid the amount demanded—£431 16s. 0d. The Dey's anger on this occasion was partly due to an idea which the merchant Gibson had carefully instilled into his mind, that English merchants were using their Mediterranean passes to cover the trade of the Dey's enemies. The truth was that when the French captured Minorca they found a number of blank passes, which they afterwards used to protect their own commerce and that of their allies.[2]

Another matter which caused the consul great trouble was that of ransoming British captives. It sometimes happened that the Algerines secured a prize with British passengers on board, and as the captain of the Algerine cruiser always took away all his captives' papers, it was impossible for them to prove that they were not in the service of the Dey's enemies. Nor were these cases tried by any recognised rules of equity. On one occasion the Dey

---

[1] C.O. 389, 49, Pitt to Aspinwall, March 15, 1759.
[2] Playfair, " Travels in the Footsteps of Bruce."

stoutly maintained that, as a certain sailor admitted to a wife in Lisbon, he must surely be Portuguese. The crews of English prizes which were taken into ports on the Bombay coast were sometimes seized by the Moors. Aspinwall secured the release of the captain and crew of a Neapolitan merchantman which had been carried to Algiers by a Gibraltar privateer and confiscated by the Dey. The Neapolitan captain looked upon his release from slavery as " little short of a miracle," and Pitt warmly complimented the consul on achieving so difficult a matter, and one which gave such satisfaction to the court of Naples.[1] Sometimes the Dey's claim proved to be correct, and when Aspinwall found a foreign vessel masquerading under British colours he took away her pass and left the impostors to their terrible fate.[2] He carefully warned seamen of British birth whom he found " skulking about these coasts in a clandestine manner and going short trips to Leghorn " that he would be unable to redeem them if they were taken by the Algerines when in foreign service. The irregularities which British privateers committed with regard to Turks they met with on neutral vessels gave the Dey a genuine grievance to balance against the consul's complaints concerning British captives. Great trouble was caused through the murder of the brother of one of the Dey's favourite officers. A British privateer had captured a Danish vessel carrying French merchandise, and with some Turkish passengers on board. When an English sailor tried to snatch a ring from one of these, he received a blow for his pains ; whereupon he drew his cutlass and killed the Turk. Aspinwall investigated the case and promised compensation, but the matter was no easy one, for the constant rise in the value of the life and effects of the

---

[1] S.P.F., Various, 68.
[2] *Ibid.*, Aspinwall to Pitt, Jan., 1757.

murdered man was only to be compared with the rapid growth of the numbers of his heirs.

On questions relating to the administration of the consulate at Algiers, Pitt showed his usual respect for businesslike methods and honest conduct. Aspinwall sent pathetic complaints to the Secretary of State's office concerning the " lack of soul and body doctors " at Algiers. He declared that he was forced to employ the Neapolitan physician to attend to such mariners and merchants, " whilst a gentleman is receiving His Majesty's pay for only walking about His Majesty's good town of London " ; and that he had had to have a child of his christened by a Greek priest, and himself been obliged to read the Burial Service at the funeral of British seamen, "because our chaplain, who enveigled and seduced by that R——l Lagorce (and enticed by his own inclinations to hunt after better preferment and ride about amongst his friends and relations in Staffordshire, where indeed there is certainly much better riding than here), has thought fit to leave us in the lurch."

Pitt enquired into both cases, gave the chaplain sick leave for twelve months, and appointed " Mr. Richard Ball to reside at Algiers as Surgeon to H.M. subjects frequenting the trade of that place," a yearly salary " to be paid to him in case of residence and not otherwise." [1]

The state of Tunis was subject to that of Algiers, but the Pasha often tried to secure independence. In 1756 the Dey of Algiers suppressed an attempt of this kind. As usual part of the victors' resentment fell upon the European consuls. By timely gifts Charles Gordon, the British consul, secured the Dey's protection, but the representatives of Sweden and Denmark were roughly handled, " very much beat, cutt and abused, their houses plundered and they almost

---

[1] C.O. 389, 49, Pitt to Aspinwall, July 14, 1760.

I

stripped naked," before they could gain the shelter of the British consulate. The Imperial and Dutch consuls and their families were carried away to Algiers as slaves.[1]

These events were a warning to Gordon to be circumspect with regard to his conduct towards the new Bey whom the Algerines had left in Tunis.

Early in 1757 a privateering question of unusual difficulty caused the consul to write to the Secretary of State for special instructions. A report was spread in Tunis that a British privateer called the *Diana* had captured the *S. Anne*, a French vessel bound for Tunis, loaded with Turkish goods and carrying Turkish passengers. It was declared that the passengers had been inhumanely treated, and their belongings confiscated and carried to Malta. The merchants of Tunis went in a body to the Bey's palace, calling loudly for justice. Gordon was summoned and ordered to freight a vessel to bring back the Turkish effects. He refused to do this, but promised to enquire into the matter, and see that the captain of the privateer was punished if he had really been guilty of the atrocious acts of murder and outrage of which he was accused. But the merchants refused to be pacified, and to appease them the Bey confined the consul to his house for a few hours. This hint induced Gordon to write a letter to Mr. Doddesworth, the consul at Malta, asking him to deliver up the Turkish effects to the bearers, two merchants of Tunis. But Doddesworth was engaged in a daily struggle with Turks who covered French trade in the Levant, and, knowing the whole story of illegal capture and cruelties to be a fiction, he told the Tunisians firmly that the question was one which the Courts of Admiralty could decide without their presence. The answer he received to this statement

---

[1] Barbary States, Tunis, 29, Charles Gordon to Fox, Tunis, Oct. 8, 1756.

caused him further to let them know " that the most respectable nation in the world was not to be made mention of impunely by any and especially an African state." [1]

When the disappointed merchants returned to Tunis the Bey declared that he would send his nephew as an ambassador to the court of Great Britain to seek for justice. In order to avoid the difficulty and expense of such an embassy, Consul Gordon promised to answer for the effects of the subjects of Tunis, and to send his chancellor to England to procure orders for their being restored. The consul took the precaution of securing a copy of the Kyma or Manifest of the goods claimed, though the Turks at first declared all the ship's papers to have been destroyed. The answer Pitt sent to Gordon's narrative of this affair is a concise statement of the firm but careful way in which the Secretary of State dealt with privateering questions.

WHITEHALL,
JULY 11, 1758.

CONSUL GORDON,

SIR,

I received and laid before the King your letter of Sept. 10 with the several enclosures, informing me of the circumstances of the capture of the *S. Anne*, a French vessel, by the *Diana*, a British Privateer. Having upon the receipt of the above letter, sent for Messrs. Nightingall Scott and Nightingall owners of the Privateer and communicated to them the violences complained of, as stated by you, I herewith enclose their answer, with other papers annexed relating to this matter.

As it is very evident from these papers that the cruelties which the Turkish passengers complained of, were void of

---

[1] S.P.F., Barbary States, 29, Doddesworth to Gordon, Malta, July 3, 1757, enclosed in Gordon's to Pitt of Sept. 10, 1757.

foundation; and as from your own account of this affair it appears that you detected the Turks in gross falsehoods, plainly calculated to support a claim to property which they never possessed, the Bey himself being convinced of their attempt to secrete the Kyma or Bill of Lading; I say, as there are so many proofs of bad faith and dishonesty in the course of this transaction, on the part of the Turks, I should think were they properly stated and enforced to the Bey, it might have satisfied him without sending your Cancelliere to London; nor can I too strongly represent the dangerous consequences of admitting any steps to be taken in matters of this nature, except such as are warranted by H.M. Courts of Admiralty whose decisions are submitted to by all Nations in the like cases. However H.M. relying upon your zeal for his service, and your prudence in avoiding as much as possible for the future, so expensive and irregular a manner of accommodating disputes, has been graciously pleased at your desire to send you by your Cancelliere Mr. Fraser a congratulatory letter to the Bey upon his accession (of which I enclose you a copy for your information) with the presents usual upon that occasion, tho' there appears no precedent of His Majesty's having paid the like compliments to former Beys; and I am commanded to signify to you His Majesty's pleasure that you deliver the said letters and presents with all proper assurance of friendship and regard.

I am, etc.,

W. PITT.[1]

The Bey had to be contented with the extortion of gifts until, in 1762, the commercial relations between Great Britain and Tunis were put on a firmer footing by a commercial treaty negociated by "Our Trusty and Well beloved Archibald Cleveland Esq. commander of one of our ships of War," who had received his instructions from Pitt the previous summer.[2]

---

[1] S.P.F., Barbary States, 29.
[2] *Ibid.*, Pitt to Gordon, Aug. 18, 1761.

With Tripoly also the Secretary of State had to deal with questions relating to trade and navigation. In 1757 Pitt was doing his utmost to bring about an alliance with Spain, and did not omit to seek the aid of the King of Naples. It therefore behoved him to give his fullest attention to a request made by Charles III that the King of England would do his best to obtain the release of seven mariners and five passengers of a Sicilian vessel which had been wrecked on the Barbary Coast. The crew and passengers had been rescued by an English merchantman and carried to Tripoly, but when they arrived in port the Bashaw claimed them as slaves in spite of the consul's argument that they were under the protection of the British flag.[1] After much trouble the Bashaw was induced to relinquish his captives out of regard to the insistence of the consul of his " Awful Great Friend the King of England."[2] In return Pitt did his best to deal justly with the Bashaw's trading subjects. He wrote strongly to the Admiralty concerning a cargo of wool belonging to Tripoly which had been unlawfully seized, and directed that steps should be taken " to prevent just cause of complaint from any of the Barbary States in amity with the King."[3] The Secretary of State also dealt adequately with a complaint made by the ruler of Tripoly that Mr. White, the British consul, was deeply in debt. He warned him plainly of " the disagreeable consequences, which must necessarily follow in case it should appear that a person, who has the honour to bear His Majesty's Commission as Consul of Tripoly, shall in any instance have availed himself of that character for purposes so very unbecoming the station in which he is placed." Finally in 1761 a treaty of peace and commerce was

---

[1] S.P.F., 69, Sir J. Gray to Pitt, July 5, 1751.
[2] C.O. 389, 49.
[3] S. P. Dom., Entry Books, 229, f. 201, Pitt to Lords of Admiralty, Whitehall, Oct. 11, 1759.

concluded with Tripoly. The last document which was received from that court at the Secretary of State's office while Pitt held the seals was a fitting comment on the economic aspect of his Barbarian policy.

" Tripoly,
    Expences of a Treaty of Peace concluded April 18, 1761."

	£	s	d
To a gold repeating watch given the Bashaw	£50	0	0
To a piece of gold brocade ,, ,, ,,	£35	0	0
To 2 cutts Scarlet Cloth cont^g. 52 yds. to do.	£54	12	0
To 3 do. given to 3 Principal Secretarys	£81	18	0
	£221	10	0

CHAPTER XI

THE SECRETARY OF STATE FOR THE SOUTHERN DEPARTMENT

PART IV

TRADE, ILLICIT TRADE AND PRIVATEERING QUESTIONS IN THE MEDITERRANEAN

By the end of 1757 the British fleet had become masters of the Mediterranean. This gave such a severe check to the trade which France carried on with Turkey, that in 1758 the merchants of Marseilles offered their woollen goods to British traders at 30 per cent. discount.[1] Some of the members of the Levant Company accepted this offer. It was not always easy for the consul to detect the fraud, as the cloth passed for French prize goods sent from Leghorn.[2] But the Levant Company passed strict regulations against the traffic, which with Pitt's aid were given the force of law by an Act of Parliament, with the result that in 1759 the annual export of French cloth to the Levant was reduced by half.[3] The same day that the Levant Company sent this joyful news to their consul at the Porte they wrote to John Evans, Esq., Commander of His Majesty's ship *Preston*, asking him to accept a chest

---

[1] Chat. MSS. 88. Heads of Case relating to the purchase of French woollen Broad Cloth by English Merchants.

[2] S.P.F., Archives, 119. The Committee of the Levant Co. to James Porter, Nov. 14, 1758. S.P.F., Turkey, 41, Porter to Pitt, May 3, 1759.

[3] S.P.F., Archives, 119. The Company to Consul Porter, London, May 4, 1759.

of plate as an acknowledgment of his great care of their ships. Dutchmen and Danes next attempted to carry on the French trade with the Levant,[1] but they fared little better than the unpatriotic British smugglers, for in the eighteenth century a neutral flag was not held to cover the enemy's goods.

Many of the Italian states were subsidised by France, and in the beginning of the war did all in their power to obstruct the action of British privateers. This hostile attitude was specially noticeable in the case of Tuscany,[2] but by the summer of 1757 the trade of Leghorn was reduced to such a low ebb that the arrival of a single prize was looked upon as an event of great importance by the Italians, whose exaggerated language showed that they had become convinced how much their welfare depended upon the navigation of the British merchant ships not being interrupted.[3] Six months later the English commerce at Leghorn was again at a stand ; a very rich convoy of merchant ships which was ready to sail for England not daring to put to sea, as they had received notice that French men-of-war were laying in wait for them.[4] The arrival of a British cruiser with seven ships laden with fish from Newfoundland " just at a time (the beginning of Lent) when there was most need for it," revived the fortunes of the English merchants at Leghorn. But the British trade did not meet the demands of Tuscany, whose inhabitants carried on a considerable trade with the French West Indies by means of English, American, and Dutch ships.[5] Tuscan colours were used ingeniously to cover French trade with the Levant. A pretended sale of ships and cargo was made by the

---

[1] S.P.F., Archives, 119. Company to Porter, London, Jan. 16, 1761.   S.P.F., Tuscany, 67, Dick to Pitt, Leghorn, Aug. 16, 1761.
[2] S.P.F., Tuscany, 64, Feb. 12, 1757, Mann to Pitt.
[3] Ibid., Mann to Holdernesse, July 12, 1757.
[4] S.P.F., Florence, 65, Mann to Pitt, June 28, 1758.
[5] Chatham Papers, 79. Extract of a Letter from Rear-Admiral Cotes, Jamaica, Feb. 15, 1760,

French owners to merchants at Leghorn, who provided a captain of their own nationality ("often a person who has never been at sea "). The government then granted colours and a pass, and the real French captain went on board as a pilot or passenger.[1]

The action of British men-of-war in stopping the products and manufactures of France found in neutral vessels caused great dismay in Tuscany, and almost ruined the French trade at Leghorn. Many difficult questions arose as to the legality of prizes. On one occasion the Regency of Tuscany objected to the testimony of a member of a ship's crew, " Geri being only a poor sailor, which is as much as to say a low man and an idiot, incapable of having a certain knowledge of what he asserted, and capable at the same time, as most of that trade are, to sacrifice the truth to any little gain." [2] France next tried to continue her trade in Genoese vessels, provided with three sets of patents and colours—Genoese to protect them from England, French to secure immunity from the Barbary Corsairs, and Jerusalem colours to enable them to enter the ports of the Levant.[3] Prussian cruisers aided their allies in stopping Tuscan vessels in the Mediterranean, and even pursued them into the Levant.

The chief trade to Naples consisted in fish from Newfoundland, and from Yarmouth, Falmouth, and other ports of Great Britain. It began in September and continued till the end of March. The ships then took in their returns of oil and fruits and sailed home.[4] In the early months of 1757 the British merchants at Naples lost nearly half their ships, and petitioned the Admiralty that a cruiser might be stationed to the south of the island of Sardinia to protect their trade

---

[1] Chat. MSS. 79.
[2] S.P.F., Tuscany, 66, Jan. 1, 1759.
[3] *Ibid.*, Consul Dick to Pitt, Leghorn, Oct. 26, 1759.
[4] S.P.F., Sicily and Naples, 15, Sir James Gray to Pitt, Aug. 2, 1757.

route.[1] Before the petition reached England the
Secretary of State had sent a fleet into the Mediterranean, which forced the French cruisers to seek shelter
in the port of Malta.[2] Venice showed favour to
British trade, and was a good market for French prize
goods from America.[3]

From the ambassador at the court of Turin Pitt
had frequent information as to the result of the act
of his cruisers and privateers upon the economic
condition of France. In the spring of 1758 the
merchants of Rochefort, Bordeaux, and Marseilles complained to the court of Versailles that of the sixty-six
vessels which had sailed during the preceding year
only three had returned by January, and that most of
the rest had been taken or sunk by English privateers.[4]
But France could give little help to her merchants.
In July the carpenters at Toulon were dismissed, and
the sailors paid five months' arrears with promissory
notes.[5] The French trade in the Mediterranean was
ruined, and in Southern France manufactures were at
a standstill, no money circulated, and the general cry
was for peace.[6] In October there was a rumour of a
quadruple alliance between France, Spain, Sweden,
and Holland. These powers, it was said, had become
convinced that their united fleets alone could encounter the British flag.[7] By the end of the year the
action of British privateers in stopping corn ships
from Italy and Sicily had reduced Southern France to
a state of famine.[8] A year later M. de Chauvelin,
the French ambassador at the court of Turin, who had
just returned from Paris, declared that France was

---

[1] S.P.F., Sicily and Naples, 15, Petition to Admiralty. Received
September 3.
[2] S.P.F., Savoy and Sardinia, 65, Turin, Aug. 17, 1757, Bristol to Pitt.
[3] S.P.F., Venice, 67, Murray to Pitt, Venice, Jan. 10, 1759.
[4] S.P.F., Savoy and Sardinia, 66, Bristol to Pitt, March 29, 1758.
[5] Ibid., July 12, 1758.
[6] Ibid., July 26, 1758.
[7] Ibid., Woodford to Pitt, Turin, Oct. 4, 1758.
[8] Ibid., Mackenzie to Pitt, Turin, Dec. 30, 1758.

" without army, without generals and without finances, that the only hopes they had left were placed in M. de Conflans' squadron, and that if that failed they had nothing remaining in which they could reasonably found one favourable expectation." [1]

After Hawke's great victory the British consul at Turin wrote to the Secretary of State that it seemed hardly necessary to trouble him with the little efforts France was making at Toulon. [2] But the Secretary of State was anxiously watching the other maritime powers of Europe, and encouraged Sir Stewart Mackenzie to send him all the information he could glean. [3] Soon he learned that the Genoese were supplying France with men and ships, [4] and that the Dutch and Sardinians were aiding her with naval stores. [5] This intelligence did not alarm Pitt unduly ; he knew that the Italian States were too poor to give efficient help, and that France was wasting her money by subsidising them. [6] He determined to continue vigorous measures, and end the war by a few decisive blows.

---

[1] S.P.F., Savoy and Sardinia, 66, Mackenzie to Pitt, Turin, Nov. 17, 1759.
[2] Ibid., Dec. 8, 1759.
[3] S.P.F., Savoy and Sardinia, 68, Pitt to Mackenzie, March 11, 1760.
[4] Ibid., Mackenzie to Pitt, June 17, 1760.
[5] Ibid., Aug. 16, 1760.
[6] Speech, Dec. 9, 1762.

CHAPTER XII

" Spain is now carrying on the worst species of war she can for France.   Covers her trade ; lends her money and abets her in negociation."—From Pitt's Speech at the Cabinet Council of October 2, 1761.

In 1825 Canning boasted that he had called a new world into being to redress the balance of the old. Almost a century before Pitt had hoped to solve the same question by the opposite method. His design was to gain a powerful commercial ally in the Old World in order to secure economic supremacy in the new.

As Secretary of State for the Southern Department Pitt had to deal with the Spanish question from various points of view. The trade between Great Britain and Old Spain was considerable, and the balance always in our favour.[1] Pitt watched this with the utmost care. The Governor at Gibraltar and the consuls at Madrid, Cadiz, Cartagena, Barcelona, Malaga, Alicante, and the Canaries kept him well informed as to the condition of Spanish finances, and constantly wrote for instructions as to the action they should take in the various disputes between British merchants and Spanish officials.[2] The most frequent complaint was that, contrary to the law of nations, French privateers were permitted to make prizes of English vessels under the guns of Spanish ports. It was also alleged that when an English

---

[1] C.O. 390, 10.
[2] S.P.F., Various, 68.

cruiser with a legally captured French prize put into a
Spanish port, the prize was often set free and the crew
of the English ship imprisoned on a charge of illegal
practices. The most famous case of this class was that
of the *Anti-Gallican*, a British privateer which had
captured a rich French East India merchantman.
The case dragged on through the first six months of
1757. Pitt sent special envoys to investigate the
matter, and did all in his power to obtain justice for
the privateer without alienating the court of Spain ;
but this was impossible. When M. Wall was pressed
on the matter he flew into a passion, and declared that
" though Spain had no troops to make her feared, she
had friends ready to receive her." [1] The threat was
hardly needed ; above all things, Pitt feared a closer
commercial union between the Bourbon powers.

The case was decided in favour of France, and,
though Pitt wrote to Sir Benjamin Keene that he was
" concerned at the conclusion of the affair," he informed the ambassador in the very same letter of the
King's strong determination to punish the licentiousness of English privateers.[2] The Secretary of State
was well aware that the privateers of his own country
often committed outrages in the Mediterranean as
well as on the Spanish Main. Consul Jordan at Barcelona reported that he had too much reason to
suspect the *Tartars' Prize* of Bristol of boarding a
Spanish vessel, and, though her papers were in order, of
robbing her master of £21 3s.[3] And when a body
of London merchants petitioned for the release of
Captain Tate of the *Duke of Bedford*, privateer, who
had been wrecked on the Spanish coast and imprisoned for illegal practices, they admitted that the
acts of which he was accused had been committed by
British merchantmen, though they declared that the

[1] S.P.F., Various, 68, Sir Benjamin Keene to Pitt, Feb. 28, 1757.
[2] *Ibid.*, 69, Pitt to Sir Benjamin Keene, Sept. 9, 1757.
[3] *Ibid.*, 68, Jordan to Pitt.

Tygress of Biddeford and the *Mercury* of Liverpool were the real offenders. Pitt treated the matter cautiously, and directed Consul Jordan " to enquire into the state of the case, and use such friendly offices for Captain Tate's assistance as may be consistent with the law and his innocence." [1]

Another group of questions that needed very delicate handling were those in which the subjects of England and Spain were jointly concerned with the Barbary States. During the Seven Years' War England was at peace with the Moors, but Spain was engaged in constant conflict with the terrible pirates who had their nests at Algiers, Morocco, and Tunis. On one occasion an Algerine cruiser seized a boat with four Spaniards in it under the guns of Gibraltar, but when her captain put into the harbour he insisted that he had no Spaniards on board and refused to submit to search. The affair was submitted to Pitt, who instructed the Earl of Home " to have particular regard to our engagements with Spain, and avoid as far as is consistent with this alienating or irritating the Algerines." [2] Finally the cruiser was allowed to sail without being searched, but the British consul at Algiers was directed to redeem the captives. Nor were these the only Spanish subjects who were delivered from the terrible fate of Moorish slavery through British intervention. Pitt instructed the consul at Morocco to do his utmost to secure the release of all Christian captives. He also bade him be " particularly careful not to supply the Prince with any arms or naval stores that may give just cause of offence to the court of Spain." [3] The Emperor of Morocco was so enraged at the refusal of the British government to supply him with arms, or the action that the consul took in protecting Spanish subjects

---

[1] S.P.F., Various, 68, Pitt to Jordan, Aug. 26, 1757.
[2] *Ibid.*, 69, Pitt to Earl of Home, Aug. 23, 1757.
[3] C.O. 389, 49, ff. 226-230, Pitt to Consul Read, July 26, 1757.

who were wrecked on the Barbary coast, that for a time he refused to supply Gibraltar with provisions. But Pitt was firm, and in the end the Dey came to terms. Though the commercial relations of England and Spain in Europe needed careful handling, the most serious causes of difference between the two nations concerned the New World. The Spanish side of the question is very simple and almost wholly economic. Spain put forward a claim to fish in the Gulf of Newfoundland which Great Britain forcibly denied. The treaty of commerce which had followed the war of Jenkins' Ear had failed to settle the old disputes about British contraband trade and the illegal seizures made by the privateers of both nations. A third grievance was that of the English settlements on the Honduras and the Mosquito Shore, and the disputed English claim to cut logwood there. The settlements were a menace to the Spanish overland trade, and if fortified might have proved very dangerous in time of war. Logwood was a valuable Spanish export, and our rights to the settlements and trade extremely doubtful.[1]

The Spanish grievances were real, and in estimating their importance it must be remembered that the eighteenth century was the age of trade wars. All the great European powers were struggling for empire, and they looked upon colonial possessions as trading posts rather than outlets for the over-abundant enterprise and population of the mother country. Thus rights of fishery, woodcutting, and navigation were very essential, and more prized by statesmen than extensive tracts of land. The Seven Years' War was a struggle for dominion rather than dominions.

Pitt did his utmost to give Spain satisfaction for her just claims ; his cruisers checked the contraband trade, and careful investigations were made as to all Spanish complaints against British privateers. In 1757 Pitt

---

[1] Clarke, "Letters from Spain," Addit. MSS.

was even willing to cede Gibraltar in order to secure a close commercial and political alliance with Spain.[1] But Ferdinand VI, who was ruled by his shrewd wife, Mary of Portugal, was resolved to develop the economic resources of his country in peace, and refused to side with either of the belligerent powers.

Two years later the accession of Charles III caused a complete change of Spanish policy. The new King was a man of fixed ideas and obstinate disposition.[2] His hostility to Great Britain is well known. The King of Spain never forgot the peremptory treatment that he had once received at the hands of a British naval officer, but his anti-English policy was influenced by national as well as personal considerations. Charles III took a keen interest in the trade and commerce of his dominions. During his reign the Spanish government itself became a huge trading company.[3] There were substantial reasons why Charles III should look with disfavour upon his great rival in the American trade, from which the greater part of his revenue was drawn. Moreover friendship with France was as congenial to the Bourbon as hostility to Great Britain was natural to the merchant prince.

In December, 1759, M. d'Abreu, the Spanish ambassador to Great Britain, presented a memorial which declared that "His Catholic Majesty could not see with indifference the English successes in America." Pitt saw at once that French influence was at work ; he noted that the memorial had been written at Saragossa, where the King was resting on his way from Naples to Madrid, "before his Catholic Majesty had reached his capital, or as much as seen the Ministers of Spain, as well as before an ambassador had been appointed for the court of England."[4]

---

[1] Chat. Corr., vol. i. S.P.F., Various, 68.
[2] Clarke, "Letters from Spain." Chat. Corr., vol. ii., p. 32.
[3] Young, "West India Common Place Book."
[4] Addit. MSS. 36807.

On December 19 Lord Bristol, who had succeeded Sir Benjamin Keene as British ambassador at the court of Madrid, wrote to Pitt that he had had a conversation with General Wall, whom Charles III had made his chief minister, in which Wall had said that his Catholic Majesty was desirous of acting as intermediary between England and France in order to establish peace within those countries. The offer was indignantly refused.

In June, 1760, D'Abreu was recalled to Spain, and his place taken by the Comte de Fuentes. The change of ambassadors was not followed by any change of policy. On June 20 Fuentes presented a long memorial dealing with the Spanish prizes taken by English privateers during the war with France, and a haughty demand for reparation. A carefully worded answer drawn up by Lord Mansfield, which fully justified the English proceedings, was returned to Spain on September 1.

On September 9 Fuentes presented two other memorials, one dealing with the fishery question and the other with that of Honduras. These documents are of the highest importance when considered as forerunners of the famous Spanish intervention of July 23, 1761. In the memorial relating to the New-foundland fishery it was stated that a similar copy had been communicated to the court of Versailles. The most pacifically minded among the English ministers were disgusted at this appeal to France in what purported to be a friendly negociation. Pitt refused to give a written answer to the court of Spain, but in his " reponse verbale " to Fuentes he declared that the King had ordered him to express his surprise and regret at the extraordinary step taken by Spain in communicating her differences with England to a court at open war with Great Britain.[1]

Pitt's fears were now fully aroused. His papers for

---

[1] Hansard, vol. xv.

K

1759 and 1760 contain statistics of the Spanish army, navy, and finances.[1] His correspondents in Old Spain informed him of naval and military preparations,[2] but what alarmed him more was information he received of a close commercial union between France and Spain in the New World. The officers of the British squadron stationed at Jamaica sent home circumstantial reports of the various ways in which the Spanish flag was used to cover the trade of England's enemies.[3] Disloyal British colonists were also concerned in this illicit commerce. By the end of 1759 Pitt's circular to the colonial governors enforced by the action of British cruisers had almost put an end to the illicit trade that had been carried on with the enemy by means of flags of truce. But in the following year this commerce found a new route through the so-called Spanish free port at Monte Christi, on the north side of the island of Hispaniola. The method by which this trade was carried on had at least the merit of ingenuity. When the English merchantmen sailed into the excellent natural harbour off Monte Christi they usually found about forty small Spanish vessels, sloops, schooners, and long-boats, who went alongside the vessels, took out their cargoes and sailed away to Fort Dauphin and Cape François, the nearest stations on the French half of the island. Here they exchanged their cargoes for French goods, sugar, indigo, coffee, and rum, and then sailed back to the English ships at Monte Christi. The merchandise was never landed at the Spanish port ; indeed, that would have been impossible, for there were no wharfs or cranes, storehouses or cellars. There was not even a custom-house ; the captains paid the governor a dollar for every hogshead of sugar they took on

---

[1] Chat. MSS. 93.
[2] *Ibid.*, and S.P.F., Various, 69.
[3] C.O. 37, 60, Rear-Admiral Holmes to Pitt, June 16, 1761.

board, and the governor's secretary superintended these lucrative but simple transactions.[1]

Pitt's European correspondents informed him that Spain was lending France money ;[2] his naval despatches proved that Spain was covering French trade, and his dealings with the Spanish ambassador at home brought home to him the fact that Spain was aiding and abetting the enemies of England in their negociations.[3]

The truth was that a brilliant idea had occurred to the Spanish ambassadors at Paris and London, which was nothing less than that of using the perplexities of France and England for the advantage of Spain. That they wished for war with England from the first is not certain, but that they had no idea of allowing France to make peace with England without the settlement of the Spanish claims is perfectly clear. It is also evident from their correspondence that they were indulging in a kind of private venture in this matter.[4] The missions of Fuentes and Grimaldi were destined to turn an indefinite understanding into an offensive and defensive alliance.

The time was most opportune ; France, once distrusted by Spain, was weak enough to be a faithful ally. The commercial union between the two countries was daily growing stronger,[5] and Spanish statesmen were fully alive to the danger of British supremacy in the Gulf of Mexico. It was with justice Fuentes exclaimed : " How critical is the present conjecture, who shall stop their conquests, if the

---

[1] C.O. 37, 60, Edward Long to Governor Moore, Dec. 31, 1760, Spanish Town Court of Admiralty. Captain Hinxman's Report, May 31, 1761, enclosed in Rear-Admiral Holmes' despatch to Pitt, May 31, 1761 (received July 22, 1761).

[2] S.P.F., Genoa, 21, Consul Hollford to Pitt, Genoa, Sept. 3, 1757.

[3] S.P.F., Portugal, 54, Edward Hay to Pitt, Lisbon, March 28, 1761.

[4] Chat. Corr., vol. ii., pp. 92, 101. Chat. MSS. 93.

[5] Chat. MSS. 93. Clarke, " Letters from Spain."

English make themselves masters of Martinico and attack Mississippi. To-day it will be at the expence of the French. To-morrow at that of the Spaniards." [1]

On July 23 Bussy presented a memorial dealing with the Spanish grievances, in which his Catholic Majesty offered to guarantee the treaty for peace pending between England and France, together with a French memorial which was couched in anything but con- ciliatory terms, and a note from Bussy to Pitt proposing the desertion of Frederick II.

Pitt gave only a "reponse verbale" as a formal answer to this astounding memorial, but he wrote to Bristol at the same time, suggesting that Grimaldi and Fuentes, who were known to be attached to the French interest, might have acted in a manner not quite in accordance with the wishes of his Catholic Majesty. This surmise Bristol was always to keep in view, and if he saw " a disposition in M. Wall to explain away and disavow the authorisation of Spain to this offensive transaction of France and to come to categorical and satisfactory declarations relative to the final intentions of Spain, he was to open to the court of Madrid as handsome a retreat as may be." [2]

All the documents Pitt returned as "wholly in- admissible." He saw at once that someone had made a gigantic blunder. Spain had unmasked her guns before the ammunition had arrived ; the threat of open hostilities had been given before the treasure fleet had reached Cadiz.

Had Pitt's ministerial position been more secure, it is probable that the presentation of the memorials on July 23 would have been followed by a declaration of war between Great Britain and Spain. But Pitt was no favourite with George III, and had many opponents in the Cabinet. To the old Whigs, men of assured

---

[1] Chat. MSS. 93 (translation of a letter in cypher received Jan. 30).
[2] Addit. MSS. 36807 and 34713.

position like Newcastle, Devonshire, and Hardwicke, it was intolerable to attend councils only to be made to acquiesce or tremble ; [1] they never forgot that a peace signed in opposition to Pitt's well-known views would mean not only the cessation of hostilities abroad, but the suspension of martial law in the council chamber. Pitt therefore waited for further evidence of the hostile intentions of Spain.   In answer to his firm but conciliatory despatch concerning the memorials of July 23, he received a reply that the presentation of the memorial of M. Bussy was a step which his Catholic Majesty would not deny had been taken with " his full consent and approbation and pleasure." The memorial made many assurances of good will, but it contained two significant passages : The King of Spain declared on his own behalf and that of the King of France that " They will never give up to England a Right which without Example it pretends to assume of hindering the one from interfering in the affairs of the other, for their mutual Assistance, as their Union, Friendship and Relationship require."

This declaration of the union of interests between France and Spain confirmed Pitt's worst fears. Wall's criticism of England's answer to the Spanish claim of fishing rights off Newfoundland was also calculated to dispel any illusions as to the possibility of continued friendship between the courts of London and Madrid : " Concerning the Liberty of the Biscayners and Giopuscoans to fish for Baccalao, an absolute Negative is given to that Right, *tho' it is well proved* and, with Respect to evacuate the Establishments, It is only offered *upon terms inadmissible* with the *Catholic King's Decorum :* that before doing it he should assure to the English the logwood. Hard proceeding certainly, for one to confess that he is gone

[1] Rockingham, "Memoirs," vol. i., p. 40 ; Addit. MSS. Brit. Mus. 35870.

into the House of Another, to take away his Jewels, and to say, ' I will go out again but first you shall engage *to give me what I went to take*' and still harder when set in opposition with the Baccalao ; *which the Spaniards want for their good as the English want logwood for their Fabricks, yet the English would by force take away the Logwood and hinder by Force the Spaniards from taking away the Baccalao.* One would think that *the English themselves might with reluctance produce such a Pretension.*" [1] It was this memorial and the letter from Bristol which accompanied it that finally forced Pitt to the conclusion that war was imminent.[2]

The Spanish despatches were received on September 11. On September 18, at a Cabinet Council at St. James's, Pitt made what even his opponents conceded was an able speech. He advised a declaration of war against Spain, and clearly stated his reasons. " Several previous steps," he declared, " showed a fixed object and system in Spain for an Union with France. The memorial from Saragossa, the Comte de Fuentes memorial, which he avowed had been communicated to the Court of France, the memorial delivered by M. de Bussy here which was returned, the intercepted letters between the Comte de Fuentes and M. Grimaldi, the Convention signed in August last between France and Spain, the Duke of Choiseul's avowal of the Convention having been begun before the first opening was sent by the Court of France for a negociation of peace." Procrastination and delay, Pitt urged, would be the most dangerous of all expedients, though he did not deny that there was danger everywhere. " They had now a total and entire avowal of the offensive step taken by France and of an entire union of Councils between France and Spain." [3]

---

[1] Addit. MSS. 36807.
[2] *Ibid.*
[3] Addit. MSS. 35870, Hardwicke Papers.

Seeing that he was to be overruled in the Cabinet, Pitt took the final step of appealing to the King. After leaving the Council, he drew up a paper in which he stated that the memorial delivered by Wall to Bristol (avowing the Spanish Intervention and declaring a total Union of Council and Interests between the two monarchies of the House of Bourbon) raised questions of such importance " that he humbly submitted his opinion to his Majesty's wisdom that orders be forthwith sent to the Earl of Bristol to deliver a Declaration signed by His Excellency to the above effect and to return immediately to England, without taking leave." [1]

At a meeting of the Cabinet Council on October 2, Pitt made a farewell speech to his colleagues. He reminded them that the war throughout had been his war ; that many of his measures, which had finally led to the greatest success, had been blamed at the outset. He reiterated his opinion that Wall's paper and Lord Bristol's letter demanded prompt action to vindicate the honour of the crown of England. " Spain," he declared, " is now carrying on the worst species of war she can for France. Covers her trade, lends her money and abets her in negociation. This puts you actually in war with the whole house of Bourbon." [2]

The exact date of the formal signature of the Family Compact may not have been known to Pitt when he made his speech at the last council ; but he knew more of its real origin and objects than a formal perusal of the document would have taught him. The compact was primarily a commercial treaty ; it guaranteed liberty of import and export for the subjects of either crown in the dominions of the other, and provided for equal treatment in all matters

---

[1] *Cf.* Articles by Hunt and Temperley on the Resignation of Pitt, *Eng. Hist. Rev.*, vol. xxi.
[2] Addit. MSS. 32928. Newcastle Papers, vol. ccxliii.

concerning trade, taxes, and navigation. By a secret
convention signed on the same day as the treaty,
Spain undertook to declare war on May 1, 1762, if
peace had not been concluded before that date.
France in return promised not to make a peace with
England that did not include satisfaction for the
Spanish grievances.[1]

By October Pitt was certain that France and Spain
were only waiting for the arrival of the Spanish
treasure fleet. War with Spain was inevitable ; if
the fleet could be intercepted it would be paid for
in advance, and with French and Spanish treasure,
not with British blood. A month after Pitt's resignation Bristol wrote to Lord Egremont, the new
Secretary of State, complaining bitterly of the haughty
language used to him by the Spanish ministers, which
he feared was due to the fact that " two ships had
lately arrived at Cadiz, with very extraordinary rich
cargoes from the West Indies, so that all the wealth
that was expected from Spanish America is now safe
in old Spain."[2]

But although he had planned the capture of the
Spanish treasure fleet, Pitt was not deceived as to
the real economic condition of Spain. In a carefully
reasoned speech on December 11, he urged the new
ministers not to hesitate to declare war on Spain.
" The revenues of Spain," he declared, " were under
£5,000,000, and she employed 70,000 men to collect
them, besides 20,000 that were engaged in the affair
of tobacco. Was this a formidable enemy ? "[3]

The war which followed verified Pitt's dictums.
Many of his partisans gave the late minister the
credit for its brilliant achievements. The capture
of Havana and Manilla was made possible by the spirit

---

[1] C.M.H., vol. vi., chap. xi., by Jean Lemoine.
[2] Addit. MSS. 36807.
[3] Walpole, " George III," vol. i., p. 8.

Pitt had infused in the British forces, but there is no evidence that he was more directly responsible for either victory.[1] Doubtless, when he urged the declaration of war with Spain, he had a scheme of operations in his mind ; he may or he may not have communicated these to his successors. In his great speech on the preliminaries for peace in 1762, he strongly censured the restoration of Havana without adequate compensation. It is almost safe to conjecture that had Pitt been in power at the time when all the trade and riches of old and new Spain lay at our mercy, he would not have been satisfied with a Manilla ransom of unpaid gold, but would have secured for Great Britain a legal share in the commerce she coveted, by a treaty sealed by cessions along the great routes of trade.

---

[1] *Cf.* Hubert Hall, " Chatham's Colonial Policy," *American Hist. Rev.*

CHAPTER XIII

THE NORTHERN DEPARTMENT

" When the Earl of Holdernesse put us off to another time, He added that as far as he was concerned, the answer was already upon paper ; that it was with Mr. Pitt to be examined and that he should soon have it back ; Insinuating to us, that without that Gentleman's avowal and approbation nothing could be done with Effect."—Extract from a letter written by the Dutch Commissaries in London to Pensionary Stein, May 4, 1759.

As Secretary of State for the Northern Department, the Earl of Holdernesse was nominally responsible for the correspondence between Great Britain and Russia, Prussia, Denmark, Sweden, the Netherlands, and the Hanse Towns. But Pitt, who had no confidence in his colleague,[1] took care that he was harmlessly employed with the formalities of his office. In these the ex-ambassador showed an acquired dexterity that had its value. Holdernesse could write a good despatch and read between the lines of an evasive reply. He received foreign ministers with dignity and entertained them kindly ; but when it came to the transaction of business he had to confess that the answer lay with Mr. Pitt.[2] Occasionally the Northern Secretary availed himself of the King's permission to efface himself at Bath while his colleague wrote important despatches to Russia or Holland.[3] Sometimes foreign ministers in England dealt directly with the Chief Secretary of State ; and the

---

[1] Stowe MSS. 263.
[2] S.P.F., Holland, 484, and S.P.F., Ministers in England, 28.
[3] S.P.F., Russia, 67, Pitt to Keith, Jan. 2, 1759, and S.P.F., Holland.

affairs of the King of Prussia always received the closest attention from the man who consistently laboured to build up a Northern alliance to counterbalance the Bourbon Compact. In fact, Pitt's policy ruled as absolute in the Northern Department as in the Southern, and Great Britain's commerce with her Baltic friends was regulated by the same principles that guided her trade with the neutral powers of the Mediterranean. It could hardly have been otherwise. Economic questions seldom allow themselves to be restrained by political geography. The Russian trade was chiefly important to Great Britain as a possible alternative to that of her American colonies. It also provided a vent for our woollen goods, and in return supplied most valuable naval stores. Our commercial disputes with Holland, Denmark, and Sweden dealt almost entirely with the trade they carried on with the French colonies in the West Indies ; and our financial dealings with the King of Prussia depended upon the prosperity of our arms in other parts of the globe. No one part of Pitt's economic policy assumes its proper proportions except in relation to the whole. It is a far cry from Quebec to St. Petersburg ; but the man who had to find a Wolfe to storm the heights of Abraham that British fishermen might possess the St. Lawrence, dare not neglect the growing French influence at the court of the Czarina which threatened our trade with the greatest of the Baltic powers.

In 1758 the immediate object of Pitt's Russian policy was to induce the court of St. Petersburg to make peace with our ally the King of Prussia. In January, Robert Keith, one of the ablest diplomatists of an age that bred statesmen rather than politicians, set out for Russia *viâ* Breslau, where he was instructed to concert measures with Frederick II. The King of Prussia was not encouraging. He told Keith that he wished him all manner of success in his mission, as

nothing could be more agreeable to him than to have
the Russians taken off his hands ; but, he said, considering the late steps they had taken, he could scarce
flatter himself with hopes of success.[1] Nor did his
mission appear more hopeful when the ambassador
arrived on Russian soil. Coming through Livonia,
he found the whole road covered with sledges carrying
corn, hay, and other provisions to the army in Prussia,
and when he approached Riga, he was again met by
" vast numbers of sledges " and some troops whom he
was told were marching to join the army intended
for Silesia. Still more ominous news awaited him at
St. Petersburg. French influence had brought about
the fall of the Chancellor Bestucheff ; and the Grand
Duchess, England's best friend, was in disgrace both
with her husband and the Empress Elizabeth. Keith
saw clearly that this was no time to enter into any
political business, and resolved to look well about him
before he committed himself in any way. He therefore coldly declined the assistance of Thomas Wroughton, an English merchant, who suggested that England
should make a bid for the favour of the future Empress
by relieving her temporary distress with a loan of
6,000 roubles.[2]

The hopelessness of the political situation forced
the ambassador to turn his attention to a secondary
object of his mission, the renewal of the treaty of
commerce between Great Britain and Russia.[3] In
this work he received much able assistance from the
British consul, Baron Wolf, one of the leading Russian
merchants whose great wealth gave him considerable
influence at court.[4] In return, the ambassador did
his best to maintain cordial relations with the members

---

[1] S.P.F., Russia, 66, Keith to Holdernesse, Breslau, Jan. 27, 1758.
[2] Addit. MSS. 35943, Keith to Holdernesse, Sept. $\frac{11}{22}$, 1758.
[3] S.P.F., Russia, 66, Keith to Holdernesse, March $\frac{3}{14}$, 1758.
[4] S.P.F., Holland, 450. Extract of a letter from Dresden, Jan. 11,
1758.

of the British factory. He listened to their grievances, ate their dinners, and upon occasions did not
even shirk a christening party and the onerous duties
of a godfather.[1]

The trade carried on by the English merchants
in Russia consisted in the exportation of hemp and
flax, linens, iron, timber, hides, wax, tallow, raw silk,
rhubarb, isinglass, and some less valuable commodities.
About three-fourths of these were paid for in bullion,
and the remainder with woollen goods, coarse cloth
for the soldiers of the Empire, and finer goods for the
Persian trade. It was estimated that Great Britain
took off as much Russian merchandise as any other two
nations, and paid more ready money every year to
Russia than all the other nations combined.[2] But so
great was the value of naval stores in 1758 that Great
Britain was exceedingly anxious to secure a renewal
of the treaty of commerce of 1734 which had expired.
By this treaty encouragement was given to English
woollen goods by equitable duties ; all mercantile
affairs in which British merchants were concerned
were made only cognisable in the College of Commerce. British merchants were allowed to buy or
hire horses and to dispose of them again. They were
exempted from the liability of having officers and
soldiers quartered upon them ; and when they desired
to return to England were allowed to do so upon
giving due notice.

At first it seemed as though Keith's task would be
an easy one. The Vice-Chancellor Woronzow himself
broached the subject of trade in one of their early
discussions, and promised that a fresh treaty should be
drafted.[3] But the fulfilment of the promise was
put off from time to time. Meanwhile there were

---

[1] Keith, " Memoirs," ed. Mrs. Gillespie Smith.
[2] C.O. 389, 31, f. 26. Report of the Board of Trade upon the Project
of a Treaty of Commerce with Russia.
[3] S.P.F., Russia, 66, Keith to Holdernesse, March $\frac{18}{28}$, 1758.

rumours that France also was negociating a treaty of commerce ;[1] and the British merchants called to mind that before the treaty of 1734 cheap Prussian cloth had undersold the superior English goods. If our ally made peace with the Empress, Silesian cloth might flood the Russian markets.[2] It was not till 1761 that Woronzow gave Keith the promised draft, and the fears of the Russia Company were verified. Almost every advantage gained in 1734 was annulled, and our trade and the personal security of our merchants placed upon the most insecure basis.[3] A counter project was returned by the Board of Trade, but the final compromise was not effected till after Pitt had been dismissed and Keith recalled.

Keith failed in the two main objects of his mission, but his stay at St. Petersburg was not without advantage to Great Britain's commercial interests. Three questions threatened the friendly relations of the courts of London and St. Petersburg : the lawlessness of the British privateers, the possibility that Pitt might send a fleet into the Baltic, and the avowed intention of Russia to colonise the lands which her armies occupied in East Prussia. Under Pitt's direction Keith managed all three skilfully. When Woronzow declared that the outrageous behaviour of our privateers gave new occasion for complaints daily, and that they had lately seized a Lubeck ship laden with valuable goods for various members of the Russian court, including two coaches for the Empress herself, Keith replied that he was exceedingly sorry for these accidents. But explained " that they were the consequence of a maritime war, where the giving of commissions to privateers was necessary ; and must unavoidably now and then fall into bad hands, as the persons who follow that trade were often not the

---

[1] S.P.F., Russia.
[2] C.O. 389, 31.
[3] *Ibid.*, and S.P.F., Russia, 68, Bute to Keith, Aug. 18, 1761.

people in the world of the best morals and strictest discipline ; but that the Government were doing everything in their power to put a stop to these licentious proceedings." [1] The Bill for the better regulating of Privateers which Pitt carried through Parliament in 1759 gave satisfaction to all the courts of Europe. The question of the possibility that Great Britain might send a fleet to the Baltic was a more delicate matter. Pitt did not wish to offend the court of St. Petersburg, but was anxious to protect the commerce of the King of Prussia. Keith disclaimed all knowledge of Pitt's intentions ; but he carefully watched the growth of a maritime union between Russia and Sweden, and the attempts of these courts to persuade the King of Denmark to join his fleet with theirs. [2] In return, the ministers of the Empress emphatically declared that their mistress had no intention of blockading the King of Prussia's Baltic ports, [3] but insisted that she would never conclude peace without some territorial compensation. This raised the vexed subject of East Prussia. As a recent writer has pointed out, though " At first sight there seems little connection between the struggle for the balance of trade and the struggle for the balance of power ; the unity becomes more obvious when we realise that increase of territory in Europe meant as much wealth to a land power, as increase of trade in America did to a maritime one. During most of the eighteenth century colonisation was even more promoted by territorial annexation than by trade." [4]

Elizabeth regarded the land her armies occupied in East Prussia in the same light as Pitt saw the

---

[1] S.P.F., Russia, 67, Keith to Holdernesse, Oct. $\frac{27}{16}$, 1758.

[2] *Ibid.*, 68, Holdernesse to Keith, Whitehall, Jan. 4, 1760.

[3] *Ibid.*, Keith to Holdernesse, St. Petersburg, March 11 / July 29, 1760.

[4] Harold Temperley, " Frederick the Great and Kaiser Joseph," p. 10. Duckworth and Co., 1915.

Dominion of Canada : an *uti possidetes* to be demanded justly at a peace as compensation for the blood and treasure so freely expended by the victorious nation. Keith made the most of the only argument he had to meet a demand so in accordance with the views of his age. He reminded the Czarina's ministers that should the Empress make a serious proposal of retain'ng her conquests in Prussia, " It would have the effect of giving just cause of jealousy to all the world ; as it would indicate clearly a Design in Russia to make herself Mistress of the Navigation of the Baltick, and consequently to engross the whole Commerce of the North." [1]

It is difficult to estimate the effect of English statecraft upon a court so variable as that of St. Petersburg. While Secretary of State, Pitt laboured incessantly to secure the safety of our Prussian ally. George III, Bute, and Egremont were content to leave him to his fate. It was the short reign of Peter III that freed Prussian soil from the levies of the Empire. Keith worked diligently to secure the renewal of the treaty of commerce, but the most important step towards this good that was made during his stay at St. Petersburg was taken by the ministry at home, in direct opposition to the judgment he had formed on the spot. In 1759 the British Consulate became vacant by the death of Baron Wolf. Keith strongly supported the candidature of a relation of the late consul's, Mr. Arbuthnot, a well-known merchant, and the friend of John Thornton and other well-known directors of the Russia Company.[2] But the Secretary of State advised the King to appoint Thomas Wroughton, whom Keith had described in 1758 as " a pushing fellow much spoilt by Sir Hanbury Williams." Holdernesse had received a hint through Denmark that this

---

[1] S.P.F., Russia, 68, Keith to Holdernesse.
[2] *Ibid.*, 67, Keith to Holdernesse, Sept. 24 / Oct. 5 /, 1759.

appointment would be pleasing to the Grand Duchess, who was wont to entrust Mr. Wroughton with her financial affairs.[1] It was a gambler's throw, for in 1759 it was impossible to foretell that Elizabeth would die in 1762, and Catharine attain supreme power by the murder of her husband.

At first Wroughton's appointment was very unpopular with the members of the British factory, and on the accession of Peter III he was removed to Warsaw ; but his policy was justified when, after Catharine's accession, a treaty of commerce was signed by Her Imperial Highness and the British ambassador at the court of St. Petersburg.[2]

---

[1] S.P.F., Denmark, Titley to Holdernesse, May 29, 1759.
[2] *Cf.* Buckinghamshire Correspondence, ed. for the Royal Hist. Scc., by Adelaide d'Arcy Collyer.

CHAPTER XIV

THE NORTHERN DEPARTMENT.—*Continued*

A VERY different scene was described by General Yorke,[1] the British minister at the Hague. Here was no despotic Empress or intriguing court. Instead, Yorke's difficulties lay with a nation of lawyers and merchants, who cared little for the rights of France or England, and were content to pursue a lucrative neutrality while the more warlike nations of Europe were cut to pieces for their benefit.[2] The French and English factions in the States-General were almost equally balanced, and although the Princess Governante[3] was strongly attached to the British interest, her support was not always an element of strength. For her throne was insecure, and those of her subjects who wished to see the Stadtholdership abolished threw in their lot with the French party, and tried to foment the commercial disputes between England and the United Provinces in order to further their own political designs. Thus, when the Princess Anne proposed a closer union with England and Prussia, her opponents found no difficulty in arousing the latent jealousy of a maritime nation by insinuating that Great Britain ntended to sweep all neutral commerce from the seas. Nowhere is the soundness of Pitt's statecraft more thoroughly demonstrated than in his treatment of this difficult question of neutrality.

---

[1] Major-General, afterwards Sir Joseph Yorke, son of Earl Hardwicke.
[2] S.P.F., Holland, 480.
[3] Anne, eldest daughter of George II of England.

His war was essentially one for and upon trade. Had he allowed Holland and Denmark to traffic with the French West Indian Islands, he would have been answerable for the miseries of a protracted and indecisive struggle. Yet a single false slip or unjust decision might have brought about a dangerous union between the neutral maritime powers. Pitt averted both calamities by skilful diplomacy backed by force. He gave law to the world, and it was a law with a sanction.

In the eighteenth century two doctrines prevailed as to the trading rights of neutrals. The great maritime powers upheld the old rule of Consolato del Mare, which had regard to the property of the goods, not the vessel, and declared that the neutral flag did not cover the enemies' goods. The smaller continental states tried to substitute the newer theory that free ships make free goods.[1] Holland, with her large carrying trade and democratic principles, supported the new doctrine strenuously. She also claimed that, by the treaty of 1674, Great Britain had guaranteed her freedom of commerce in time of war ; but set aside this pretension when reminded that she was also bound by treaty to send military aid to Great Britain if an enemy landed in the British Isles. During the Seven Years' War the dispute between England and Holland passed through various phases. The Dutch shifted their ground from time to time, but the real source of difficulty was a question of colonial rather than international policy. In the eighteenth century commerce between a neutral state and the colonies of a belligerent was generally understood to be contrary to the law of nations. As has been seen, all the great powers of Europe sought to monopolise the trade of their colonies. When war broke out, the

---

[1] *Cf.* Lecky, " History of England in the Eighteenth Century," and Fitzmaurice, " Life of Shelburne," vol. ii., p. 74.

enemy refused to allow neutrals to carry on a traffic from which they were debarred in time of peace. The crux of the whole matter was the point at which the theory and practice of eighteenth-century colonial policy met and clashed. In theory the mother country controlled the trade of her colonies. In practice they carried on a large illicit commerce with her rivals. Thus, when Pitt had forced the Dutch to give up their claim to trade directly with the enemy's colonies, there remained the difficult question of the trade carried on with the French West Indian Islands through the Dutch settlements of St. Eustatia and Curaçao. The story of the dispute is of necessity somewhat rambling because of the varying nature of the claims put forward by Holland. But it illustrates the extraordinary difficulty of the question of neutrality, and the justice with which the English prize courts dealt with the causes brought before them.

At the beginning of the war French agents were busy in Dutch trading towns, engaging merchants to trade with the French West Indian Islands. In 1757 Dutch merchants made large profits, and in the following year, though the insurance had risen to 15 per cent. on the outward bound and 34 for the homeward, many of the great houses of Amsterdam and Rotterdam were content to risk their ships on voyages to St. Domingo and Martinique.[1] Pitt's cruisers soon checked this illicit trade by stopping all Dutch vessels suspected of being concerned in it, and carrying them into British ports, where, if the cargo was proved to be French, it was condemned. Unfortunately, the smaller British privateers, until restrained by the Act of 1759, sometimes exceeded their instructions, and committed acts of violence which verged on piracy. Loud outcry was raised in Holland. Every imaginable kind of complaint was

---

[1] S.P.F., Holland, 480, Yorke to Holdernesse, Feb. 17, 1758.

laid before Yorke at the Hague ; while M. Hop, the Dutch minister in England, never failed to entertain Holdernesse at least once a week " with a variety of disagreeable topicks." [1] Sometimes the grievance was that British privateers robbed and plundered Dutch ships in the Channel, at other times the want of redress in the Admiralty courts, or that any of their ships should be visited or stopped at all upon any pretence whatever. The reply made by both ministers was the same, and carefully framed in accordance with the rules that Pitt had laid down for the treatment of neutrals. [2] The only redress against the alleged violence of privateers was by the regular course of law and justice. If proof could be brought, the King's servants would take care that a criminal process was carried on against the delinquents, and they would be punished with the utmost severity as pirates. Holdernesse remarked that vague and unfounded stories of the excesses of privateers had been circulated upon the 'changes of Rotterdam and Amsterdam, and contributed more to the clamour against the English than other points of a more difficult nature. The chief of these he aptly described as " the proper bounds that ought and must be set between interrupting the real fair trade of the Dutch and suffering them to carry on the trade of the enemy that passes the Bounds of the Neutrality they profess." This subject led naturally to the question of the right Great Britain claimed of visiting Dutch ships at sea, and effectually preventing them from supplying the French colonies with necessaries, and carrying on for them a trade which they could not themselves support in time of war, and to which the Dutch were not admitted in time of peace. This was a point on which Pitt declared that he would never

---

[1] S.P.F., Holland, 481, Holdernesse to Yorke, July 21, 1758. This admirable despatch gives a careful account of the whole question.
[2] Addit. MSS. 32883, Newcastle to Yorke, Sept. 5, 1758.

yield, and when it was broached to Lord Anson he became " furious," and said that if we gave it up we should be undone, and that the Dutch might as well protect the French army by giving them Dutch colours.[1]   Holdernesse was directed to reply that it was the frauds of the Dutch merchants, the falsity of their sea papers, their double invoices, double passports, and false clearances that occasioned that strict examination, and that these were the real reasons why they avoided the English law courts, where their transactions would be brought to light.   And in accordance with the definite instructions of his court, Yorke informed the Pensionary that the King, his master, was " determined to prevent the French American trade from being carried on by other powers, under specious pretences of Neutrality, and not let the chicane of words be worked into a Permission to carry on a trade with the Enemy, which tho' not enumerated as a specific article of Contraband, becomes so to all intents and purposes by particular Circumstances."   The Pensionary said at once that this declaration would alter the course of the deliberations in the States-General concerning a resolution sent up by the merchants of Holland.   Yorke thought it wise to give the impression that he had heard only a vague report of this affair, but sent Holdernesse a copy of the resolution that he might see the gulf that diplomacy had to bridge.[2]

The strong assurances given by Great Britain that the licentiousness of her smaller privateers should be checked pleased the Dutch merchants.   But when the Princess Governante proposed that her land forces should be augmented, the French party, led by Amsterdam, protested formally against any such action ; and, in order to divert the attention of the

[1] Addit. MSS. 32885, Newcastle to Yorke, Nov. 17, 1758.
[2] S.P.F., Holland, 481, Yorke to Holdernesse, Aug. 1, 1758.

nation, did all in their power to increase the clamour against England. Holland had demanded an equipment to protect the West Indian trade ; some of the other provinces tacked the augmentation on to this, and refused to give their consent to one without the other. The Princess was thus placed in a most difficult position. She could not go back upon the augmentation question without dishonouring herself in Europe, and losing all her credit in her own country ; and yet if some compromise were not effected with England she ran the risk of being thought to abandon the trade and navigation of the republic to the rapacity of English privateers. The complaints of the merchants were swelled by the evident distress to which the families of many citizens had been reduced by the interruption of their trade. The fact that in most instances the breadwinners had been peculating in an illicit traffic made no difference to the popular outcry. The Dutch even talked of coming to a rupture with England, and declared that they were not stronger when they shook off the Spanish yoke, and that they would follow the example of the King of Prussia, who, though the ruler of a small state, defended himself against a multitude of foes. Yorke was convinced that those who were the hottest for war would be the first to wish it ended, but feared that the enemies of the House of Orange might unite themselves with France in order to free themselves from the Stadtholdership.[1] Notwithstanding the gloomy view of the British minister at the Hague, Pitt remained firm on the question of the right of search. But he took infinite pains to secure the release of some Dutch ships from Surinam which had been brought into port by British privateers. The peculiar wording of the Prize Act of 1757 complicated the matter, and Pitt finally decided to compensate the captors with a draft on the Treasury

---

[1] S.P.F., Holland, 481, Yorke to Holdernesse, Aug. 29, 1758.

for £1,000.[1] Hardwicke declared that the effect produced in Holland was well worth the sum,[2] and Newcastle admitted that Pitt had done well.[3] Pitt, himself, had no hope that Dutch merchants would give up trying to cover French West Indian trade, and was determined to frustrate their designs by force. Yet he was resolved to keep the rules of warfare and maintain strict discipline among the privateers. He did not expect an accommodation with the Dutch, but he laboured ceaselessly to prevent an open rupture. When the Princess Royal sent him a message of thanks for the release of the Surinam ships he replied :

" Very many and great difficulties remain to be surmounted, nor is it to be hoped that this old source of Disputes and Ill-will (in all wars) can be quite closed ; but if these waters of bitterness can be kept, by the Wise and Honest in both countries, from entirely overflowing, it is enough to preserve the Union of the Two nations and to prevent the overthrow of the System of Europe." [4] Newcastle believed that the affair might be amicably settled if Pitt would give way a little. Yorke feared the worst if he did not. But events justified Pitt's actions and prediction.

The proprietors of the colony of Surinam waited upon Major-General Yorke several times to express their appreciation of the speedy justice that had been done them ; and the States of Holland agreed to change the destination of the ships with which they had intended to cover the trade to the French Islands, and use them solely for the protection of the trade of their own colonies.[5] At this moment an unfortunate

---

[1] Addit. MSS. 38883, Newcastle to Yorke, Sept. 1, 1758.
[2] *Ibid.*, Hardwicke to Newcastle, Sept. 3, 1758.
[3] *Ibid.*, Newcastle to Yorke, Sept. 12, 1758.
[4] *Ibid.*, 32884., Copy of a letter from Mr. Secretary Pitt to Major-General Yorke, dated St. James's Square, Sept. 29, 1758.
[5] S.P.F., Holland, 482, Yorke to Holdernesse, Sept. 8, 1758.

incident threatened the growth of friendly relations. One of the Surinam ships was retaken in the Channel by the *Ulysses* privateer, and though the mistake was speedily rectified, a bad impression was made at Amsterdam and Rotterdam. And Dutch merchants declared they would not risk their ships at sea while the King of Great Britain could not control his own privateers. The Princess Governante did all in her power " to assuage the heats that had arisen," and was so successful that on September 26, 1758, Yorke wrote home that the Exchanges in all the trading towns were then as eager for an accommodation as they had been for a rupture at a time when they believed neutrality would mean ruin. A resolution of the States-General passed the day before spoke of their ships trading *de bonne foi*, which implied that they had given up the case of those which masked the trade of our enemies. Yorke urged strongly that now was the time to effect an amicable compromise. But the affair was one of great difficulty, and a month later he wrote again, begging that some definite rules might be laid down as to the exact nature of the trade allowed to neutrals, and more stringent measures taken to prevent illegal acts on the part of British privateers. He pointed out that : " Whilst the clamours all arise from our Superiority at sea, and the consequence of it, and that it costs nothing to France to cajole them, we must expect that we shall lose ground and the authority of the Stadtholder come to nothing, unless some regulation is entered into and Measures taken to prevent these parts of their complaints which we ourselves disapprove." [1]

Pitt called three Cabinet meetings to discuss the resolution passed by the States-General and the complaints of the Dutch merchants. At the first it was decided to make concessions to the Dutch if they

---

[1] S.P.F., Holland, 482, Oct. 17, 1758.

would give up the French trade ; at the second
Lord Holdernesse was directed to take minutes of the
debate, and with Lord Hardwicke's assistance to draft
a despatch from them.[1] When Parliament met,
Alderman Beckford brought up the question of the
Dutch disputes, which were a matter of grave concern
to the city fathers. Pitt replied that " very unjust
acts had been done by our privateers, that we ought
to be just and to detect and punish those, and then not
to suffer the Dutch to break their neutrality by illegally
carrying French property. But that as France had
suffered by her Extended ambition, so we the Mistress
of the ocean should use our power with moderation."[2]
On November 28 the Cabinet met again, " when the
great letter was produced." Newcastle reported to
Yorke that " Mr. Pitt has done extremely well in the
affair." It was decided that a separate letter with
conciliatory promises should accompany the official
despatch.[3] George II also wrote affectionately to
his daughter.[4] Holdernesse sent the letters away on
December 30. The official despatch dealt exhaustively
with the whole question, promised redress for acts of
violence committed by British privateers, but insisted
on the right of search, and maintained that all the produce of the French colonies was contraband. In the
separate and secret letter Yorke was reminded that
" you that reside in Holland, hear but one side of the
question, and are only witness to the animosity these
disputes occasion there ; at the same time it is but
too true that the Resentment against the Dutch for
their partial proceedings and fraudulent practices
is very great upon the 'change of London, and begins
to spread itself universally, so that in every light
whatsoever it is highly to be wished that this trouble-

---

[1] Addit. MSS. 32885, ff. 365 and 461.
[2] *Ibid.*, ff. 524-526.
[3] *Ibid.*, 22886, f. 98.
[4] *Ibid.*, f. 68.

some affair were happily and speedily ended." [1] The Princess Royal was alarmed at the strong resolutions contained in Holdernesse's office letter. On the evening of the day she received it she wrote to the British minister : " You know as well as me, my good Yorke, what unreasonable people we have to do with, and that next week all our enemies will be in aray expecting to take fire, if there is not some hope of redress offered." [2]

George II was much disturbed by his daughter's fears ; Pitt immediately ordered a list to be prepared of ships detained in British ports which were not suspected of being concerned in the French colonial trade, and after much difficulty secured the release of four of them by compensating the captors out of the prize money fund. [3] The Princess Royal was " much pleased and comforted " by Pitt's " obliging " words and actions, but before she received news of either she and her " good Yorke " had to weather the impending storm.

On December 7 a deputation of forty-six Dutch merchants arrived at the Hague, waited upon Her Royal Highness and made her a violently anti-British speech, copies of which their servants afterwards distributed about the town, not forgetting to affront the English minister by leaving one at his door. This remarkable document complained bitterly of Mr. Pitt's strong statements to M. Hop about the Dutch disputes and the West Indian trade. Pensionary Stein assured Yorke that this paper had been composed by people who had become violent through their sufferings, and by no means contained the sentiments of the State. [4] But the habit of petitioning is infectious,

---

[1] S.P.F., Holland, 482, Dec. 5, 1758, Yorke to Holdernesse.
[2] *Ibid.*, Dec. 5, 1758.
[3] Addit. MSS. 32886, f. 431, and 32887, Jan. 5, 1759, Newcastle to Yorke.
[4] S.P.F., Holland, 482, Yorke to Holdernesse, Dec. 8, 1758.

and the shipwrights of Saardam followed suit by
forwarding a request to H.R.H. that they might be
exempted from paying taxes because they were ruined
by England.[1]   When the States of Holland assembled
many more petitions were presented, " requiring Protection, deputations to England, and every other
Proposition the heated Imaginations of these Clamour-
ous Sollicitors could invent, to resist which it requires
no ordinary Share of Temper." [2]   However, Yorke
continued to talk the language of diplomacy, and told
the Pensionary that he was ready to confer with the
deputies of Amsterdam and to hear what they had to
say.   He hoped by this means to make the representatives of the town, which really decided commercial
questions, commit themselves either for or against the
measure, and relieve the Princess of the odium of the
affair.   The meeting took place at the Pensionary's
house, and the deputies appeared extremely pleased
at the attention paid them.   Yorke explained that if
they would give up their claims to cover the French
West Indian trade (which he " very roundly told
them, they should never be permitted to carry on
while Great Britain had a ship at sea ") their lawful
commerce should be secured to them.   " After much
mumbling the thistle " they declared themselves
content, but said that the question of contraband
needed explanation.   At a second meeting Yorke
explained his fear that the islands of St. Eustatia and
Curaçao would try to carry on the trade with the
French islands, and the deputies confessed that it
would be almost impossible to prevent this, as these
colonies subsisted upon the illicit trade they carried
on with both French and Spaniards as well in time of
peace as of war, but declared that the States were
ready to give up their claim to this traffic.[3]

---

[1] " Separate and Secret " letter of same date.
[2] *Ibid.*, Yorke to Holdernesse, Dec. 15, 1758.
[3] S.P.F., Holland, 482, Hague, Dec. 29, 1758.

The New Year brought fresh difficulties to our minister at the Hague. On January 5 he wrote home that " the Danish minister had joined in the general cry against the conduct of Great Britain at Sea." The probability of a defensive union between Denmark and Holland was a serious matter ; and both Pitt and Anson believed in the possibility of a French invasion of Great Britain countenanced and supported by the Dutch.[1] The death of the Princess Royal on January 12 lessened the British interest in Holland for a time. Four days later William Bentinck explained to the Duke of Newcastle in a private letter that though the direct trade to the French colonies in America would be given up :

" The trade to and from our own colonies and establishments ought to remain untouched and uncontrouled and whatever is brought from thence in Dutch bottoms ought to be considered as Dutch property and fall under the Denomination of Free Ship, Free Goods. Give me leave to tell you that our Islands, I mean S. Eustatia and Curacao are worth little and Curacao particularly not worth sixpence, to the Republick without the Clandestine Trade carried on between English, Spaniards, French and Dutch contrary to the Treatys. The Great Profit of your trade in America arises from the Smuggling trade in, and with the Colonies or Establishments of other Nations, which trade, tho' prohibited, it is not possible to prevent. This is a fact better known to you, than to us. And I may, I believe venture to say that Jamaica, tho' so much more considerable in itself is much in the same case as our colonies." [2]

On January 26 Yorke forwarded a memorial to the same effect from the States-General. He knew it would be inadmissible to the ministers of George II. Yet he urged them not to be discouraged at the ill success of his negociation, as he was convinced that Holland still

---

[1] Addit. MSS. 32886, f. 376, Newcastle to Yorke, Dec. 19, 1758
Ibid., 431, " Memorandums for the King," Dec. 22, 1758.
[2] Addit. MSS. 32887.

desired to live on friendly terms with Great Britain.[1]

The Secretary of State replied that the Resolution of the States-General gave His Majesty the deepest concern, " as it asks everything and grants nothing ; and which besides the false way of Reasoning it contains and False Facts it alledges, is wrote in a manner very different from that plain modest, yet nervous style, in which the Resolutions of the States used to be drawn." Yet, as Yorke had declared that the Pensionary and the wiser sort of people disliked and disavowed this inflammatory performance, a counter project was returned.[2]   As the year wore on the British successes at sea made the Dutch " a little more prudent than they were formerly not to strain the cord too hard."[3]   But in March the Rotterdam merchants again became violent, and threatened to send a formal deputation to England, to send one likewise to Denmark, to propose a defensive alliance, and to join twenty-five men-of-war to theirs, to recall their seamen from abroad on pain of death and to prohibit all English manufactures.[4]   Yorke was not unduly alarmed, for he knew that " these people tho' they would have others go at full Gallop, never can be made to go faster than their natural amble."[5]   After much wrangling among themselves, the States agreed to send three commissaries to England to watch the progress of their litigation with Great Britain. M. Boreel of Amsterdam went as an accredited minister, M. Van de Poll as his assistant. M. Meerman, the Pensionary of Rotterdam, belonged to the violent party, and was sent to keep a jealous eye upon the more pacific Amsterdammers.[6]

They arrived in London on April 9, and three days

[1] S.P.F., Holland, 483.
[2] Chat. MSS. 89, Draught to General Yorke, February, 1759.
[3] Addit. MSS. 35482, Yorke to Keith, Feb. 13, 1759.
[4] Ibid., 32888, Yorke to Newcastle, March 6, 1759.
[5] Ibid., 32889, Yorke to Newcastle, March 13, 1759.
[6] Ibid., f. 199.

later waited upon Lord Holdernesse. Early the next week they had their first private audience with George II. No business was discussed at these visits of ceremony, but the deputies set to work at once to discover the attitude of the British nation towards the Dutch disputes, and to judge for themselves as to the justice of the decisions of the Courts of Admiralty. They found the British merchants as clamorous as the Dutch, and formed a very favourable opinion of the laws and justice of Great Britain. At first they had some difficulty in proceeding with their negociation, because Pitt was ill at Hayes and Holdernesse was forced to confess that he could do nothing without the sanction of his chief. Meanwhile the deputies saw something of English life. They were taken to Oxford to see the installation of the Chancellor, and to Richmond to inspect the King's gardens, which they declared were " kept like Madame Van der Meer's but much better." They spent a day at Claremont and paid a visit to Tunbridge Wells, " to pass the time and see the life there." Boreel reported that the King was very gracious to him, and that the Queen and the Princesses seldom passed him unnoticed. The Yorke family were kind, and Lord and Lady Holdernesse charmed the deputies by their " distinguished " hospitality.[1] The time was not wasted. Boreel was a shrewd man, and he saw beyond the sights. He caught a glimpse of a proud nation ruled by a hardworking aristocracy of birth and culture, who had nothing to gain or fear from the general public. He was amazed to find that when " the common people cried out that the Dutch were as bad as the French, the ministers took no notice of them. In Holland such popular clamours would have produced violent resolutions in the States-General. In England they passed

---

[1] S.P.F., " Foreign Ministers in England," 28, Boreel to Madame Boreel, London, May 15, 1759.

unheeded, and the ministry proceeded to an act of justice in direct opposition to vulgar prejudices."[1]

Fortunately Pitt got the better of his gout in time to support the Bill for the better regulation of Privateers, which came before Parliament in May. He returned to town in very good humour, " agreed " with Newcastle, " charmed " Holdernesse, " pleased " Hardwicke, " went down to the House of Commons furious for the Prize Bill," and made a " manly and honourable speech " which carried the day.[2] The disorders most complained of by the neutral powers had proceeded from the action of small privateers, a class of vessel which by the new Act were excluded from receiving letters of Marque to prey on the enemies' trade. In future this work could only be carried on by large ships financed by wealthy merchants or corporations, who would be made responsible for any illegal acts committed by their sea captains. After May, 1759, the dispute between England and Holland concerned the interpretation rather than the violation of maritime law. The most serious difficulty was the illicit trade to the French colonies carried on by the Dutch through their own islands. Before Boreel had been many weeks in England he agreed with Pitt that it was hopeless to expect the question would ever be settled, and that the diplomatists' task lay rather in preventing a standing grievance from becoming a *casus belli*. He reminded his critical friends in Holland that :

" 'Tis a very different thing to make conventions or to chat by the fireside in the Council Chambers. If people are not content at the Hague ; Be so good as to take my part in particular, and to assure everybody that we spare no labour, pains and application to assist the Merchant, and to keep the two powers together, in order to prevent the ruin of both."[3]

---

[1] S.P.F., " Foreign Ministers in England," 28, Boreel to Madame Boreel, London, April 27, 1759.
[2] Addit. MSS. 32890, ff. 193 and 484. *Ibid.*, 32891, f. 5.
[3] S.P.F., " Foreign Ministers in England," 28, Boreel to M. Bacher, May 22, 1759.

The presence of the Dutch commissaries in London undoubtedly made for peace and harmony. The question was whether the hasty tempers of their masters at the Hague would stand the strain of a protracted negociation. George II tried to sound Boreel on the matter by asking when his wife was coming over. Boreel replied that he did not know, as a member of his family was ill, but confessed to his wife, " to speak plain Dutch to you, whether we are to stay, or to return home, is what I cannot tell, nor shall be able to guess in some weeks yet."

Thanks to the Dutch minister's tact and Pitt's forbearance the deputies stayed a year, and returned to the Hague full of commendations of their treatment in England. It was not said at the Hague that they had been recalled, but only that they had leave to return upon their private affairs. Boreel came back as ambassador, and maintained the Dutch interest in England wisely and honestly. After the year of victory, Pitt's cruisers policed the Atlantic and enforced the letter of the law. But the old source of disputes could never be quite closed, and broke forth with added bitterness in the great struggle in which the American colonies gained their independence.

CHAPTER XV

THE commercial disputes between Great Britain and Denmark were of a less complicated nature. The Danish government quickly abandoned their claim to carry on a direct trade with the French West Indian Islands, but protested against the interruption of their commerce with their own colonies, and also against the violence of certain British privateers who pillaged and ransomed their ships.[1] Walter Titley, the British minister at Copenhagen, explained that these last were criminal matters which his government detested and disclaimed, and for which the perpetrators would undoubtedly be punished when discovered.[2] The subject of the French goods which the Danes were accustomed to smuggle through their colony at Santa Cruz, and which Pitt declared to be contraband in time of war, was more difficult. Santa Cruz was a fruitful island, very different from the " Rock " of St. Eustatia. It was reasonable for the Danes to wish to bring home their own produce, natural for them to continue to smuggle French goods, and difficult for British cruisers and privateers to distinguish between fair and illicit trade. The results were long cause lists in the Courts of Admiralty, and serious delays and interruptions to Danish commerce. The ministers of both countries were anxious to keep the peace,

---

[1] S.P.F., Denmark, 104, Goodricke to Holdernesse, Copenhagen, Dec. 23, 1758.
[2] *Ibid.*, 105, Titley to Holdernesse, Jan. 6, 1759.

and proposed ingenious solutions to the problem.
Titley suggested that presents might be used occasionally with good effect, but urged that " a much more
effectual way should be tryed to carry our point.
As these two Northern Crowns are now so passionately
bent upon Trade, the more we get the Keys of that
into our power the more we shall be respected by
them ; so that, if, on the occasion of any Difference
with the Emperor of Morocco we could resume
Possession of Tangier and thereby become absolute
masters of the Streights of Gibraltar, we should have
little reason to mind what ministers might be employed
or what schemes pursued either in Denmark or
Sweden." [1] Bernstorff, the able Chancellor of Denmark, made a more practicable suggestion. He proposed that when a Danish ship was carried into a
British port for examination she should be released
as soon as security had been given for the amount
in litigation, in case the judgment went against the
owner. [2] It was not expected that this indulgence
would be given to ships suspected of carrying certain
contraband stores. Pitt sanctioned this expedient,
and did all in his power to secure speedy justice for
Danish traders. Denmark was able to maintain her
neutrality, and Great Britain carried on her Baltic
trade unmolested.

Sweden's attitude towards Great Britain was hostile
from the beginning of the war. Objections were
made to every minister whom Great Britain proposed
to send to Stockholm. One, who had been born in
the British factory there, was declared to be a native
of Sweden, who could not be received as a minister
of a foreign power ; [3] another was refused admittance
to the country because he had paid a visit to the King

[1] S.P.F., Denmark, 103, Copenhagen, July 15, 1758.
[2] Ibid., 105, Titley to Holdernesse, Copenhagen, Jan. 23, 1759.
[3] S.P.F., Prussia, 71, Holdernesse to Mitchell, Feb. 25, 1758.

of Prussia on the way.[1]   In 1758 Sweden joined her
fleet to that of Russia, and threatened to blockade
the King of Prussia's Baltic Ports.[2]   Pitt referred to
Sweden as " that little teazing incident."   She was
not strong enough to hamper his plans seriously ; but
the ministers of Great Britain did not forget that the
Queen of Sweden was a Prussian ; here also it was
suggested that presents might be used with good effect.[3]

The story of the relations between Great Britain
and Hamburgh and the Hanse Towns during the
Seven Years' War reads rather like a quasi-historical
farce.   But it was no joke for those who played their
part upon this little stage.   In their attempt to please
both England and France the men of Hamburgh
suffered materially.   Messrs. Hanbury and Halsey,
members of the British factory at Hamburgh, held
the commission from England of remitting the money
to His Majesty's army under the command of Prince
Ferdinand of Brunswick.   They usually sent the
money down the Elbe by way of Haarburgh ; and had
arranged to despatch casks of silver and gold to the
amount of £30,000 sterling on April 1, 1760.   Fortunately the night before they received information
that an armed boat was laying in wait within the booms
of the city, ready to seize the British supplies.   The
strange craft omitted to make the usual entry at the
Custom House, was stopped, and upon examination
found to contain " Ten blue Regimentals turned up
with yellow, and two with red, Twelve Laced Hats,
Ten Muskets, One Hand Gun, Nine Cutlasses, Four
Swords, a Packet of Gun Powder and Shot, and another
containing flints." [4]   The crew consisted of three men,
who declared that they had been employed by one

---

[1] S.P.F., Denmark, 103, Titley to Holdernesse, Copenhagen, July
15, 1758.
[2] *Ibid.*, 104, Goodricke to Holdernesse, Aug. 22, 1758.
[3] *Ibid.*, 110, Holdernesse to Sir John Goodricke, Whitehall, Jan. 23,
1761.
[4] S.P.F., Hamburgh, 77, April 4, 1760.

Nagant, a tobacco merchant who lived at Hamburgh, and was "a born subject of the Prince of Liege." The sailors swore that all they knew of the affair was that they had been told to wait some distance from Hamburgh, where they would be joined by some more boats with an officer from whom they were to receive their further orders. The British minister at Hamburgh raised a great outcry at the violation of the neutrality of the Republic and the privilege of the Free Steam, and demanded that Nagant should be exemplarily punished. M. Champeaux, the representative of France, claimed both boat and effects as belonging to the King, his master, and threatened that if they were not returned the Hamburgh ships in French ports would be retained. Nagant was imprisoned, but soon released, and swaggered about the city, declaring that he carried the patent as Commissaire de la France in his pocket.[1] Choiseul was not contented with the lapse of the prosecutions against his agent, and persuaded Louis XV to annul his treaty of commerce with Hamburgh because his boat and arms had not been given up. The Hamburghers sent deputies to Paris to request a renewal of their treaty of commerce, which they did not obtain till they had given a substantial guarantee for the correctness of their future behaviour.[2]

The affairs of our ally, the King of Prussia, engrossed a large share of the attention of the Secretary of State for the Northern Department, and were carefully supervised by Pitt, but they have little direct bearing on colonial matters. The question of the subsidies paid by Great Britain to Prussia can only be usefully dealt with as an item in the finance of the war, a subject which has been treated exhaustively by a recent writer.[3] Pitt's subsidies were sufficient, but not extravagant,

---

[1] S.P.F., Hamburgh, 77, June 17, 1760.
[2] *Ibid.*, June 24, 1760.
[3] Basil Williams, " Life of William Pitt."

and the Great Commoner took care that he got value for the nation's money. A solitary incident bearing on the question of neutral commerce is to be found among the English state papers which deal with the affairs of Prussia during the Seven Years' War. In a letter to Holdernesse, dated December 11, 1759, Sir Andrew Mitchell relates that :

" In the Month of May last one Thomas Pearn (that had served as Masters Mate on board His Majesty's ship the *Union*, and afterwards on board the *Duke William* Cutter, from which he was discharged by order of Admiral Smith) came to the Prussian Army, whilst they were passing the Mountains into Moravia pretending to be sent by some Merchants of Yarmouth to sollicit leave to fit out ships under the Prussian Pavillion, but as he did not succeed in his Negociation, and besides appeared to be crazed, I thought it then unnecessary to trouble your Lordship."

---

[1] S.P.F., Prussia, 72.

CHAPTER XVI

THE STAMP ACT

" The true cause of the discontent of the Americans has arose from the rigour and hardship of the Stamp Act. It stands upon a principle that it is politic to call upon the plantations to pay a perpetual revenue ?and tax in aid of the Mother Country.
" Now the true connection between the colonies and Great Britain is commercial."—Lord Camden, in the debate in the House of Lords on the second reading of the Bill for the Repeal of the Stamp Act, March 11, 1766.

THE Stamp Act is the supreme test of Pitt's economic theories and colonial policy. In the early months of 1766 he spoke with unrivalled knowledge and mature judgment. His generous behaviour after the events of 1761 had given men confidence in his criticisms. No longer could he be accused of desiring to embarrass the party in power for private ends. His personal ambition was half satisfied and consciously limited. During the last years of the reign of George II, Pitt had ruled a kingdom and won an empire. After 1761 he knew that he could never regain the position he had lost. Sir William Pynsent's bequest had removed that desire for the emoluments of office which might have influenced Pitt as husband and father. Finally, the disease which often crippled his limbs had not yet impaired the vigour of his intellect. Unshackled by office, party, or faction, Pitt spoke with the scientific detachment of an expert. The dictum of 1766 must not be confused with the rhetoric of 1739.

The Stamp Act problem was one which could only be solved by a statesman who possessed an intimate knowledge of American affairs. It was no petty

quarrel over colonial liability for the war debt, but a
question which concerned the fundamental principles
of the complicated commercial and political systems
by which England governed her plantations.   There
is as much history as politics in most of the Stamp
Act speeches ; they abound in references to charters
and appeals to precedents.   This line of argument
appears at first to obscure the real points at issue ;
but though pedantic in form it is scientific in spirit,
for the quarrel between Great Britain and her colonies
started when the *Mayflower* sailed from Plymouth.
The New Englanders owed both the strength and the
weakness of their provincial character to early adversity.
Driven from one country by religious bigotry, they
suffered bitterly while wresting homes from the hostile
inhabitants of another.   The descendants of the
Pilgrim Fathers were not the sons of good citizens,
but of men who had worked out their own political
salvation.   A sturdy race developed self-reliant but
suspicious, narrow with the zeal of conviction.   In the
eighteenth century, when England began to take a
tardy interest in her colonies, she tasted the bitter
fruits of ill-treatment and neglect.   The suspicions
of the colonists made the governor's work irksome
and ineffective ; while the mutual jealousy between
the different provinces made any united effort against
their common enemies almost impossible.   It was the
continual sordid struggle over supplies between the
colonial assemblies and their governors that induced
Sir William Keith to submit a proposal to George II
that a revenue should be gained from America
by a tax on stamped paper.   Sir William Keith had
been Deputy-Governor of Pennsylvania for many
years, and the " Short Discourse on the present state
of the Colonies in America with respect to the Interest
of Great Britain," [1] which he presented to the King

---

[1] Brit. Mus. King's MSS. 205, f. 46.

in 1728, is remarkable not only as being one of the first Stamp Act schemes, but also for the light which it throws upon the respective points of view of the English government and the colonists. Keith wrote as a man divided against himself; all through his address it is easy to trace the conflict in the writer's mind between what he felt the colonial attitude towards the mother country ought to be and what he knew it to be. He began his memorial with a careful exposition of the economic beliefs of the correct governor of his day, declaring that :

"Every act of a dependant provincial Government ought to terminate in the advantage of the Mother State, unto whom it owes its being, and by whom it is protected in all its valuable priviledges ; hence it follows that all advantageous Projects or commercial gains in any colony which are truly prejudicial to and inconsistent with the Interest of the Mother State must be understood to be illegal and the practice of them unwarrantable because they contradict the end for which the colony had a being and are incompatible with the terms in which the People claim both Priviledge and Protection."

With delightful irony he continues :

" Were these things rightly understood amongst the Inhabitants of the British Colonies in America there would be less occasion for such instructions and strict prohibitions as are daily sent from England to regulate their conduct on many points, the very nature of the thing would be sufficient to direct their choice in cultivating such points of industry and Commerce only as would bring some advantage to the Interest and trade of Great Britain ; they would soon find by experience that this was the solid and true foundation whereon to build a real interest in the Mother Country and the certain means to acquire Riches without envy."

After this interesting dissertation, the ex-governor proceeded to " take a short view of the principal benefits arising to Great Britain by the trade of her colonies." He noticed the colonial consumption of

British woollen manufactures, linen and calicoes;
and that the demand for British household furniture,
trinkets, and East India goods was growing as the wealth
of the colonists and their taste for luxury increased.
The colonial returns were also a source of wealth to
Great Britain, especially tobacco, which helped to
balance the unprofitable trade with France. The
increase of shipping and seamen which enabled Great
Britain to carry great quantities of fish to Spain,
Leghorn, and Portugal, and furs, logwood, and rice
to Holland, was deemed doubly advantageous by the
strict mercantilist, who further advocated "reasonable encouragement of colonial production of such
naval stores as timber, hemp, flax, pitch, tar, oil, resin,
copper ore, pig and bar iron, whereby the balance
of trade to Russia and the Baltick might be much
reduced in favour of Great Britain." But the
enthusiasm of the mercantilist could not quite overcome
the fear of the ex-governor, who saw in the mother
country's policy of securing to herself a monopoly of
" the superfluous cash and other riches acquired in
America not one of the least securities that Great
Britain had to keep her colonies always in subjection."

When he reached the real point of his address, Keith
wrote with a lively memory of his former struggles
over supplies with his worthy friends in Pennsylvania.
He declared that all he had said about the improvements of the plantations would signify very little
unless a sufficient revenue could be raised to support
the necessary expenses of government, for which purpose he proposed that a duty might be placed on
stamped paper and parchment in America.

It may be that this was the proposal that Walpole
said he would leave to a braver man. It is noteworthy
that Keith next presented his memorial on December
17, 1742, after Walpole's fall.[1] In this memorial

---

[1] Addit. MSS. 33028, ff. 376, 377.

Keith argued that the war with Spain had forced England to fortify her colonies and aid their westward expansion, and that therefore the colonies were bound to pay for this help and protection. In fact, the arguments brought forward by the ex-governor in 1742 were the same as those urged by English ministers in 1755.

During the war of the Austrian Succession, the colonists fought bravely with little help from the mother country; and when they saw their interests ignorantly sacrificed by the restoration of Louisburg to France in 1748, they were naturally both discouraged and enraged. In 1754 the chronic border warfare between the French and English colonists in North America again assumed the proportions of a national struggle. At home the Duke of Cumberland designed Braddock's ill-fated expedition ; in America the colonial governors proposed a congress at Albany to discuss some scheme of union by which the colonists might be able to direct their united strength against their enemies.

The necessity of the foundation of a central fund for the great struggle just opening was admitted by governors and colonials.[1] Governor Shirley of Massachusetts urged the plan for a general union upon his council and assembly in the strongest terms.[2] Dinwiddie did the same in Virginia. Dr. William Clarke, of Philadelphia, declared that although several of the English governments were singly a match for the French, yet all of them together would be weaker than the enemy.[3] Dr. Franklyn, in his reply to Clarke's letter, told him that he thought his observation as to the fatal disunion among the colonists was just, and expressed the fear that unless the English colonies made a united and vigorous effort the French in time

---

[1] *Cf.* H. E. Egerton's " Short History of British Colonial Policy."
[2] Addit. MSS. Brit. Mus. 35909, ff. 176-179.
[3] Mass. Hist. Soc. Coll., series i., vol. iv., p. 74, May 6, 1754.

would become sole masters of the continent. At the congress at Albany the Indian Chiefs told their white brothers some home truths as to their weakness and lack of union; [1] but the " red " man's philosophy made no impression on the colonists, whose hearts were hardened by their governors' rhetoric and temper. After their failure at this attempt at voluntary co-operation, the governors turned their thoughts to coercion. Not even Franklyn questioned the sovereign legislative power of the British Parliament. Might not a tax be levied by the supreme power ? As early as July 24, 1754, Governor Dinwiddie had proposed to Sir Thomas Robinson that an Act of Parliament should levy a general poll tax of half a crown on all the colonies to raise a fund for the expedition. [2] The Board of Trade, in their report on this proposition of August 9, 1745, declared that : The union was so necessary and the advantages that it would secure to the colonies so apparent that they hoped the colonies would put no difficulties in its way. If such difficulty should arise they maintained it would be necessary to settle the question of the supplies for the campaign by the authority of Parliament. [3]

The bare hint of direct taxation raised a storm of opposition in the colonies. The colonial point of view has often been misunderstood ; too much stress has been laid on the constitutional side of the question, and even this has been judged by English standards. The jingle of the catchwords " taxation " and " repre-sentation " is confusing to Englishmen of the twentieth century. They are apt to forget that the theory of representative government in the eighteenth cen-tury differed much from that of our own day, and that the colonial point of view was distinct from both.

---

[1] Mass. Hist. Soc., series iii., vol. v.
[2] Hardwicke Papers, Addit. MSS. Brit. Mus. 35907, f. 186.
[3] *Ibid.*, ff. 189-193.

In all cases the symbols are the same, but the values are different.

The colonials objected to direct taxation by the mother country for two reasons. In the first place, they believed that they contributed their fair share to the burden of imperial defence in respect of the advantage which the mother country gained through the direction of their commerce. Secondly, they feared that if a revenue were forthcoming from the colonies it would be used to defray the expenses of colonial government. Thus the colonial governors, always hated and distrusted by the majority of the colonists, would be made independent of the legislative assemblies. Benjamin Franklin expressed the colonial point of view admirably in his letter to Governor Shirley of December 4, 1754. Shirley had written to Franklin to enquire his opinion of that part of the Albany scheme which the governor described as " the Proposal of Excluding the American assemblies from the choice of the Grand Council and taxing the people in America by Parliament." [1] Franklin began his reply with a little poke at Shirley's correct official attitude. " In matters of General concern to the People and especially where Burthens are to be laid upon them, it is of use to consider as well what they will *be apt* to think and say, as what they *ought* to think." He went on to describe the loyalty of the people and their readiness to grant supplies, and touched delicately on the prevalent opinion :

"That Governors often come to the colonies merely to make fortunes, with which they intend to return to Britain, are not always men of the best abilities and Integrity, have no estates here, nor any natural Connections with us, that should make them heartily concerned for our welfare ; and might possibly be sometimes fond of raising and keeping up more Forces than necessary, for the profits accruing to themselves, and to make

---

[1] Addit. MSS. Brit. Mus. 35911, ff. 60-61.

Provision for their Friends and Dependants. That the Coun-
cellors in most of the Colonies, being appointed by the crown,
on the recommendation of Governors, are often of small
Estates, frequently dependant on the Governors for offices
and too much under Influence. That there is therefore great
reason to be jealous of a Power in such Governors and Councils,
to raise Such Sums as they shall judge necessary by Draft on the
Lords of the Treasury, to be afterwards laid on the Colonies
by Act of Parliament, and paid by the People here ; since they
might abuse it, by projecting useless expeditions harrassing
the People and taking them from their labour to execute such
Projects, and merely to create offices and Employments, gratify
their dependants, and divide Profits."

The colonists even feared that if a tax could be laid
on them by Act of Parliament for the support of their
governments, their assemblies would be dismissed as
a useless part of the constitution. The New Englanders' fear of a strong central government was
enhanced by the example they had always before
them of Montcalm's efficient military rule in Canada.
They dreaded lest the constitution proposed at Albany
should put the English colonists " on a footing with
the Subjects of France in Canada, that now groan under
such oppression from their governor, who for two
years past has harrassed them with long and destructive marches to the Ohio." [1]
Yet, though the colonists were unwilling to make any
great sacrifice for a system of united defence, they were
much alarmed when they heard that the mother country was considering the policy of keeping a standing
army in America. In 1755 William Bollan, the agent
for Massachusetts at the court of Great Britain, sent
home an alarming piece of news : " that it was
intended by some persons of consequence that the
colonies should be governed like Ireland, keeping up
a body of standing force with a military chest there,"

---

[1] Addit. MSS. Brit. Mus. 35911, ff. 60-61.

and that their legislative powers should be abridged
" so as to put them on the same foot as Ireland standing by Poynings' law." There is no reason to doubt
Bollan's information, which he said he had gathered
in the House of Commons from some significant
words the Speaker let slip in conversation about the
clause for extending the Mutiny Bill to provincial
troops.[1] The fear that the mother country might
be enabled by raising direct taxes either to make the
governors independent of their assemblies, or to
invest the supreme legislative power in America
either in some Grand Council in America or in the
Privy Council of the mother country, influenced the
Americans more than any vague speculative ideals
of Sovereignty and Right.

The colonists also objected to paying a tax to Great
Britain for the simple reason that they were sufficiently
taxed already. In 1754 Franklin declared that,
besides the taxes necessary for the defence of the
frontiers, the colonies paid great sums to the mother
country unnoticed :

" For Taxes, paid in Britain by the landholder or artificer,
must enter into and increase the price of the produce of the
Land, and of manufactures made of it ; and great Part of this
is paid by consumers in the colonies, who thereby pay a considerable part of the British Taxes. . . . In short we are not
suffered to regulate our trade, and restrain the Importation
and Consumption of British Superfluities (as Britain can the
consumption of foreign superfluities), our whole wealth centers
finally among the Merchants and Inhabitants of Britain, and if
we make them richer, and enable them better to pay their
taxes it is nearly the same thing as being taxed ourselves and
equally beneficial to the crown." [2]

Pitt endorsed this view when, twelve years later, he

---

[1] Hist. Soc. of Mass. Coll., series i., vol. vi., p. 129, William Bollan to
Josiah Villiard, Secretary of Mass.
[2] Addit. MSS. 35911, f. 61.

reminded the House of Commons of the profits that accrued to Great Britain from her colonial trade :

" I will be bold to affirm that the profits to Great Britain from the trade of the colonies through all its branches is two millions a year. This is the fund that carried you triumphantly through the last war. The estates that were rented at two thousand pounds a year, three score years ago, are at three thousand pounds at present. Those estates sold then from fifteen to eighteen years purchase ; the same may now be sold for thirty. You owe this to America ; this is the price America pays for her protection."

The great war that broke out in 1756 made the Albany strife appear mean and petty. Events soon proved the wisdom of the advice of the Indian chief who had warned the English to stop their bickerings and prepare for a death struggle. The Seven Years' War brought matters to a crisis in rather a curious way. Pitt saved the American colonies, but the success of his war policy almost ruined them. By 1759 England had gained that command of the Atlantic upon which all Pitt's schemes of conquest depended; incidentally his cruisers had put an end to the illicit trade between English, French, and Spanish colonies. England's commercial regulations had long been irksome to her colonies ; when wholesale evasion became impossible the system was felt to be unbearable.

After the peace of 1763 the colonies were exhausted, discontented, and secure from French invasion. The position was critical, but not desperate. All the colonies needed was a little wholesome neglect ; the mother country should have remembered that her plantations were but children states, whose undisciplined natures had been strained to the utmost, but whose constitutions were essentially hardy. It did not need the genius of Pitt to deal with such a situation. The incompetence of Newcastle would have done equally well, but Grenville's plodding industry was fatal ; all that it achieved was the contraction of two debts, one for the value of the United States of America, the other for £631 9s. od. The latter is endorsed " American Stamp Office Law Bill," [1] and the first entry is dated " Trinity Vacation, 1763," for hardly had a packed Parliament approved the peace of Paris before Grenville burnt his fingers with an act which Walpole had left to a braver man. The scheme that Grenville adopted was one which a certain obscure Mr. McCulloh had submitted to the Government in 1755. The plan was most carefully considered. Grenville's lawyer had long interviews with McCulloh, and took down careful notes of the needy adventurer's great scheme of Imperial finance. It would have been better if Grenville had consulted the crafty Franklin, who would have reminded him that when it was a question of imposing financial burdens it was more important to consider what people were apt than what they ought to think.

The colonial opposition to the Stamp Act of 1765 might have been predicted in England in 1763, for it took the line already marked out by the objections to the Albany scheme of 1754. There were several Englishmen in 1765 who understood the American point of view. Shelburne, who was president of the Board of Trade, knew all about the commercial nature of the tie that bound the colonies to England, described his speech in the House of Lords on the motion for the repeal of the Stamp Act of 1765 as an endeavour " to distinguish the real ties by which America might be supposed to hold to this country in order to obviate objections arising from a thousand false lights thrown out on this subject ; acknowledging the power of parliament to be supreme, but referring the expediency of the act to be considered in a commercial view, regard being had to the abilities of Americans

---

[1] Addit. MSS. 35911, ff. 18-37.

N

to pay this tax and likewise to the consequences likely
to proceed in any event from the late violences." [1]

Shelburne sent an abstract of this speech to Pitt,
who replied in a letter which he had composed very
carefully, making a rough draft first :

> " The line your lordship took the first day in the House of
> Lords, I should have been proud and happy could I have held
> pace with in the House of Commons, being under the strongest
> conviction that, allowing full force to all the striking topics
> for upholding, in the present instance, the legislative and execu-
> tive authority over America, the ruinous side of the dilemma
> to which we are brought is, the making good by force there,
> preposterous and infatuated errors in policy here : and I shall
> unalterably sustain that opinion." [2]

Parliament reassembled on January 14. The King, in
his speech from the throne, declared " that he had lost
no time, on first advice of these disturbances in America,
to issue orders to the governors of his provinces, and
to the commanders of his forces, for the exertion of all
the powers of government, in the suppression of riots
and tumults, and in the effectual support of lawful
authority." [3] Pitt made his first Stamp Act speech
in the debate which followed the address. Historians
whose opinions differ widely on other material points
are agreed as to the authenticity and importance of
the speeches Pitt delivered at this crisis.[4] They have
their own place in English history and literature;
on such a subject appreciation is presumptuous and
criticism futile. All that is attempted here is to lay
stress on those portions of Pitt's speeches which deal
with his commercial policy and reveal his intimate
knowledge of the American point of view; and to

---

[1] Chat. Corr., vol. ii., p. 353, Shelburne to Pitt, Dec. 21, 1765.
[2] *Ibid.*, 359.
[3] *Ibid.*, 363.
[4] *Cf.* Frederic Harrison's " Chatham," p. 159 ; Sir George Trevelyan's
" American Revolution " ; and Lawson Grant's " Chatham's Colonial
Policy."

draw attention to two recently discovered debates, one of which contains a speech by Pitt, and the other a careful exposition of the commercial nature of eighteenth-century imperialism.

In his speech on January 14, 1765, Pitt reminded the House of Commons of the great benefit England reaped through the colonial trade, the price that America paid for her protection. He expressed it as his opinion that the whole commercial system of America might be altered to advantage, and his closing words contain an appeal to the commercial good sense of his countrymen.

" Will you quarrel with yourselves, now the whole House of Bourbon is united against you ?   While France disturbs your fisheries in Newfoundland, embarrases your slave trade to Africa, and withholds from your subjects in Canada the property stipulated by treaty ; while the ransome for the Manillas is denied by Spain."

His peroration gives a clear exposition of his Imperial creed :

" we may bind their trade, confine their manufactures and exercise every power whatsoever except that of taking their money out of their pockets without their consent."

From January 14 to January 28 numerous petitions dealing with American affairs were presented to the House of Commons. Some of these throw a good deal of light on the controversy, for they show the attitude of the English merchants trading to America towards a question which concerned them very nearly, and upon the commercial nature of which they could speak from practical knowledge. They were all agreed that the Americans were unable to pay both for English luxuries and the Stamp Act. Many merchants declared that if they received American orders while the Stamp Act was in operation they would shorten their credit. Some said they would only send goods which were paid for in advance. All maintained that specie was very scarce in America, and that the colonists were discontented with the regulations which interfered with their trade with the Spanish possessions.[1]

A committee of the whole House sat from eight to ten hours almost every day till February 21, when they presented their report in the form of seven resolutions. The first of these declared that :

" The King's Majesty, by and with the consent of the Lords Spiritual and Temporal, and Commons of Great Britain, in parliament assembled, had, hath and of right ought to have, full power and authority to make laws and statutes of sufficient force and validity to bind the colonies and people of America, subjects of the crown of Great Britain, in all cases whatsoever." On February 3 this declaratory resolution was proposed by Conway to the House of Commons in committee. While insisting on the legal right, Conway spoke sympathetically of the American grievances he had just been investigating. He admitted that the Americans were irritated by repeated blows at their trade and property, the restrictions on their trade in lumber and molasses, the irritation caused by the interference of the swarms of cutters, the exhaustion and debt caused by war. Colonel Barre moved an amendment " to leave out the words in all cases whatsoever." Pitt rose to second the amendment. He tried to distinguish between the powers of legislature and taxation, but reached surer ground in his peroration, which gives a flashlight picture of the American Empire which he had designed :

" America was of mean beginnings, so was Rome, but the scanty fountain is now become a large stream covered with sails and floated with commerce, and nothing shall prevent my using an effort beyond my force to avert the Dangers of such an express and full

---

[1] Addit. MSS., 33030, f. 87.

declaration. I think you have not the right I mean to waive it by silence, and most magnanimous exertion of power is often in the non-exertion of it. I wish this to be an Empire of Freemen : it will be the stronger for it and it will be the more easily governed. Let the premises and consequences agree therefore, decline the right, do not let lenity be misapplied or rigour unexecuted : take not the worst of both. The colonies are too great an object to be grasped but in the arms of affection." [1]

The debate in the House of Lords of March 11 has also a peculiar interest. It shows the great Whig oligarchy of the eighteenth century discussing the affairs of the nation whom they hoped they had excluded from their councils. The noble lords, having cleared the House and gone into committee, spoke freely even of the conduct of the Commons.

In the eighteenth century the House of Lords was a meeting-place for the chiefs of political clans, men whose political power was only equalled by their zest for affairs of state. The debate is a clear exposition of the colonial policy of the age. Lord Camden tersely summed up the gist of many previous speakers' expositions when he said, " Now the connection between the colonies and Great Britain is commercial." On a closely allied point there was a consensus of opinion ; no one denied that the balance of the trade with the colonies was in England's favour. The Duke of Grafton put the case concisely. " It is said that America is not taxed—I answer they pay taxes in taking your manufactures." The Duke of Richmond declared roundly that the principle of the Bill was absurd—" that America should be taxed, for since the balance of trade with America was in our favour, it was obviously ridiculous to take away from the colonists the money with which they were to pay the balance."

---

[1] *Amer. Hist. Rev.*, April, 1912. Debates on the Declaratory Act and the Repeal of the Stamp Act, 1766.

Lord Shelburne, who at this time was acting in close union with Pitt, described the principles of his speech as " all commercial."

Meanwhile the Americans were watching the actions of English statesmen with the greatest care. Pitt and Shelburne were regarded as the staunchest friends of the colonies. George III was suspected of wishing to enslave a free people, and Bute was if possible more detested and despised in America than in England.[1] The colonists had suffered so much at the hands of incompetent court favourites in high positions that they overrated Bute's power and influence. They regarded the Repeal of the Stamp Act as a healing measure, but the wound still smarted. A learned divine of Boston, writing to a friend in England on November 14, 1766, expressed the Americans' feelings concisely.

" We in America are perhaps more obliged to our friends in Great Britain, who raised a spirit among the people, than to the Parliament which repealed the Act which was calculated (I do not say designed) to enslave the colonies." [2]

On July 30, 1766, William Pitt became Earl of Chatham and Lord Privy Seal. His term of office lasted nominally till 1768, but the ministry was Chatham's only in name. His later years were spent in retirement, and with regard to his colonial policy are important only as showing that his unwavering opposition to any scheme for taxing the colonies was based on a true appreciation of the American point of view, which was primarily commercial. The colonists regarded Chatham's new title as an indication that he was falling under court influence; they feared that " Mr. Pitt the great Patriot, who seemed formed to stem the torrent of corruption, had been gained over

---

[1] " Archives of Maryland," vol. vi. Corr. of Gov. Sharpe, vol. iii., p. 258.
[2] Hist. Soc. of Mass. Coll., series iv., p. 400, Letters from Andrew Eliot to Thomas Hollis.

by the Northern thane." They mourned over his fall the more because they believed him to be the only man capable of putting things right between Great Britain and her colonies—because he had the confidence of both.[1] The people of Boston would hear no ill of Mr. Pitt, whom they were slow to learn to call Lord Chatham, though they spoke no more of the statue they had proposed erecting to him.

Townshend's tea duties were received by the colonists with ominous calm. Thomas Cushing, the Speaker of the Massachusetts Assembly, tried, through the influence of Lord Shelburne, to gain relief from what he described as "the difficulties our trade labours under." Cushing declared that the people of Massachusetts desired a strict union and harmony with Great Britain; he deplored the action of those pernicious busybodies who tried to sow discord by representing "the colonies as setting up for independence, as turbulent, factious and disloyal," and the mother country as "disposed to treat the colonies with severity, and to deprive them of their most valuable rights and privileges." His objections to the duties were merely a temperate official reiteration of the objections raised in 1754 and 1765.

"As to imposing duties, so long as they are confined to the regulation of trade, and so conducted as to be of equal advantage to all parts of the Empire, no great exception can be taken to it ; but when duties are laid with a view of raising a revenue out of the colonies, and this revenue also to be applied to establish a civil list in America, and by this means (as the report goes) the Governor, the Lieutenant Governor, Secretary, Judges, etc., are to have their salaries first from home and paid out of the monies that shall be from time to time collected by virtue of Act of Parliament already passed or to be passed, and it is apprehended cannot be done without vacating our charter, and in effect overthrowing our present constitution." [2]

---

[1] Hist. Soc. of Mass. Coll., series iv., p. 400, Letter from Andrew Eliot to Thomas Hollis, May 13, 1767.
[2] Mass. Soc. Coll., iv., series iv., p. 348.

In April, 1768, the merchants of all the American colonies came to an agreement not to import British goods for twelve months ; they imagined that by this means they would so distress the British merchants that they would become their " greatest and warmest advocates." Much was hoped from the new ministry, and the people of Boston were very disappointed when they heard the King's speech, and " the echo of the Lords and Commons," to find that they were " exceedingly high against the Town and Province." With reason the colonists asked, " What can the ministry propose further ? We have troops, we do not resist them. The duties unreasonable as we think them are paid without opposition. Perhaps the town has not in everything acted with that prudence that might be wished, but what could be expected from a people struggling for liberty and made desperate by the measures taken with them ? " When the citizens of Boston were told that Parliament might offer to receive their representatives, they naturally asked :

" Will they incorporate us, and allow us free trade as they allowed Scotland ? If they do, they will soon lose the trade of the colonies, who can purchase much cheaper elsewhere. If they do not, we shall not think we are upon an equitable footing." [1]

The Americans had no wish for representation ; all they desired was the repeal of the revenue acts and the withdrawal of the troops. There was some division of opinion among the colonists as to whether they ought not also to insist upon the repeal of the Declaratory Act. Cushing was among those who urged that this was more than the colonists could expect from Great Britain, and that the demand might bring about a premature rupture with the mother

---

[1] Mass. Hist. Soc., series iv., Thomas Cushing to Dennys de Berdt, April 18, 1768.

country, which it was to the interests of the colonists
to avoid, since if they only bided their time their
natural increase in wealth and population was certain
eventually to settle the dispute in their favour.[1]

Chatham, who corresponded both with Cushing
and his English correspondent, the philanthropic Mr.
Hollis, was thoroughly conversant with the American
point of view, and on February 1, 1775, he presented
to the House of Lords his "Plan for settling the troubles
with America," of which Lord Sandwich said, " I can
never believe it to be the work of any British peer.
It appears to me to be rather the work of some
American." [2]   This was high though unintentional
praise.   The plan, roughly outlined in a fit of illness,
was not a finished production, but it went to the root
of the matter.   It provided for a congress " in which
the colonists should vote supplies for imperial uses
other than the usual charge for support of civil government in the respective colonies."   While the legislative
power of Great Britain was declared to be supreme,
the fears of the colonists were to be soothed by the
declaration :

" that no tallage, tax or other duty for His Majesty's revenue
shall be commanded or levied from British freemen in America,
without common consent, by act of provincial assembly
there duly convened for that purpose."

This plan must be judged on its merits, not as a
great Imperial scheme, but as a rough temporary
expedient hastily sketched out by a master-hand to
meet a pressing difficulty.   Its chief merit was that
it suggested, but did not dictate.   Americans declared
that all would yet be well " if those high points about

---

[1] Mass. Hist. Soc., series iv., Thomas Cushing to Arthur Lee,
September, 1773.
[2] Quoted by Mr. Lawson Grant in his " Colonial Policy of Chatham,"
Queen's Quarterly, 1911.

the supreme authority of Parliament were to fall asleep." Could Pitt have lulled the restless spirit of his age, they might not have awakened till his dream had become a reality and England with her colonies had formed "An Empire of Freemen."

APPENDIX
UNPUBLISHED LETTERS, ETC., BY WILLIAM PITT

APPENDIX

S.P.F. Portugal 51.

Pitt to Hay, relating to the revival of an old law forbidding the extraction of bullion.

WHITEHALL.
NOV. 7TH, 1759.

MR. HAY,

SIR,

Your letter of the 2nd April, was laid before the King together with the copy of the Sentence of the Court of Relacam passed on the 26th of Dec. last, and the Memorial of the Merchants relating thereto. And I am commanded by the King to acquaint you that His Majesty sees with much regret the indispensable and only medium of the Ballance of Our Trade with Portugal not only brought again into Discussion, but so severe a Sentence pronounced, and notwithstanding your repeated Representation, finally confirmed by His Most Faithful Majesty with regard to a seizure of some Money in the publick streets of Lisbon so long ago as the year 1755, which sentence appears to be founded on the Extension of an old Penal law contrary to the usual method immemoriably practised in all preceeding cases of a similar Nature and particularly to what happened on occasion of a like seizure made in the year 1752 when the King sent Lord Tyrawly to Lisbon which money was restored to the Proctors of Mr. Charles Theobald the person from whom it had been taken ; The King hoped that equitable and recent Determination would have been made a rule for the Future and therefore His Majesty could not but receive with much surprize the account you

transmit of the Sentence now passed which has so justly
alarmed all His Subjects concerned in the trade with Portugal
and must if drawn into Example greatly interrupt if not
render all commerce between the two nations totally impracticable by not only exposing the persons of His Majesty's Subjects
to immediate danger but by depriving them of all possibility
of receiving the Ballance due to them from the Portuguese
and also subjecting them to vexatious seizures and tedious
and expensive law suits to be decided on the evidence of the
meanest sort of people, who are entitled to half the sum con-
tested, and consequently are too deeply interested in the issue
of the suit to be by the acknowledged Rules of Equity admitted
as the only or principal Evidence and that too in their own
cause, the present case also most certainly demands the higher
attention from the Circumstances you so properly observe
viz. *that this sentence will stand as the Example to all future ones,
all the old Law suits upon seizures having been burnt in Novr. 1755.*

In this situation the King cannot refuse to His Subjects
that Interposition in their Favor and that Protection which
they so justly and so earnestly implore ; I am therefore to
signify to you His Majesty's Pleasure, that you should, in the
King's name, make the most serious Representations on this
Subject to the Count d'Oegras, a Mr. Da Castia and such other
of the Portuguese Ministers as you shall judge proper and set
before them in the strongest light the many ill consequences
that the least extension of a Penal Law may be productive of,
and particularly how nearly the equitable, and till now invariable construction of that in question, must affect the nature
and essence of all Commercial Interests, that great Foundation of Friendship, and true Bond of Union, which has so long
and so happily subsisted to the mutual Benefit and Advantage
of Both Nations. The King has however that firm reliance
on the Known Justice and Equity of His Most Faithful Majesty
and the Portuguese Ministers have themselves so frequently
acknowledged the many and great benefits arising to their own
country from their Trade with Great Britain, which they have
more than once owned cannot be carried on without the
Extraction of Gold ; that His Majesty is persuaded when they
shall cooly reflect on the consequences of not only an Extension
but even too rigid an Execution of a Law made 400 years ago,
they will not hesitate to take such measures as may effectually

quiet the minds of the British Factory, by entirely removing
the alarming apprehensions they at present labour under, and
fixing, for the time to come, the Commercial Interests of the
two nations on a solid and permanent Basis, so that His Majesty's
subjects may obtain, without any vexation or difficulty what
shall be justly due to them on the Ballance of their trade with
Portugal, which can alone restore that Mutual Confidence
so absolutely necessary in all commercial affairs ; you will at
the same time give the warmest assurances to the Portuguese
Ministers of His Majesty's invariable desire to maintain and
cultivate the most perfect harmony with the Court of Lisbon,
and you will express the King's concern to see any Incident
arise, that may if not Timely prevented, produce in its Consequences, any uneasiness between the two nations. You will,
in a proper manner, acquaint the Factory at Lisbon, of the
King's Gracious attention to their Representations and assure
them that they will never fail to meet with such support and
Protection from His Majesty as their complaints shall require
and as the Nature and particular circumstances of the case
shall admit.

I am, etc.,
W. PITT.

S.P.F. Portugal 52.

Pitt to the Earl of Kinnoul.

WHITEHALL
MAY 30TH, 1760.

. . . . .

Your Excellency will, then, express, that it is a most sensible
consolation to His Majesty to consider, that the unprosperous
state of the affairs of France affords, at present, the justest
grounds to believe, that however unfriendly her disposition towards Portugal may be Providence will not put into the hands
of that haughty but impotent court the means of carrying such
malignant designs into effect.

. . . . .

Nor indeed can the equity and wisdom of the Spanish
Councils leave room to suppose, that the Court of Madrid
would adopt from France, such dangerous suggestions of

injustice and oppression; or that Spain, at the instigation of a power actuated by Despair would wantonly stain the beginnings of a reign with Designs of most flagrant, and odious, violence, and, by rashly embarking on new and vast projects (of which she would never be likely to see a successful end) commit to the Hazard of precarious events, Her important and favourite possessions in Italy, not yet sufficiently secured against the probable and obvious views of Austrian ambition.

· · · ·

That the King will ever consider the Defence of the Kingdom and Dominions of Portugal, the ancient and natural ally of England as an object dear to the Honor and Welfare of His Crown and People, next in degree to the very preservation of the British Dominions themselves.

· · · · ·

The present state of my health obliges me to defer to another opportunity writing to your Excellency on the very important subjects of our Commercial affairs with Portugal, and particularly on the matter of the several exclusive Companies for carrying on the Trade to the Portuguese Settlements, mentioned in your separate letter of the fourteenth past, for a due understanding of the nature, and Limitations whereof, I must necessarily desire Your Excellency to send me more ample and circumstantial Lights and Informations.

S.P.F. Portugal 52.

Pitt to Kinnoul.

WHITEHALL.
JUNE 24TH, 1760.

· · · · ·

Your Excellency is so sensible that the long memorial transmitted in your separate Letter, relating to the Exclusive Companies for the Brazils, is of a Nature to require such thorough and mature deliberation, before a Resolution can properly be taken thereon, that you will not expect me to enter at all, at present, into that complicated and extensive consideration.

S.P.F. Portugal 53.

WHITEHALL.
SEPT. 30TH, 1760.

Letters received.

. . . . .

And as there does not arise out of them occasion of transmitting to Your Excellency any further Instructions from His Majesty with regard to the several important Commercial objects committed to your care, and concerning which you seem by your last letter in hopes of soon receiving answers from the Court of Portugal; I have only to express my sincere wishes that those answers may be satisfactory, and that Your Excellency may have the credit of bringing things to a happy Conclusion, within the Short Period, which was from the beginning allotted for your Residence at Lisbon.

S.P.F. Portugal 53.

Kinnoul to Pitt.

OCT. 29TH, 1760.

. . . . .

As soon as it was known that I was to leave this place, several gentlemen of the Factory were very importunate with their committee to know what had been done, and accordingly a meeting was appointed.

. . . . .

I permitted the consul to acquaint them that I had presented memorials upon two points and had received very lately answers to them which would be transmitted to His Majesty's Secretary of State. That the King of Portugal had granted a revision of the sentences, which confiscated the money seized in the streets: that the Answer relating to the Authority of the Judge Conservator contained strong assurances of His Most Faithful Majesty's favourable dispositions towards all the King's Subjects residing in His Dominions; but that as no specifick Order was to be made in consequence of this Answer, I did not think myself at Liberty to communicate the Particulars of it until it had been laid before His Majesty. The Factory ordered a deputation to attend me with their thanks and

O

compliments. The Committee who have in the whole course of their transactions behaved with great discretion and Moderation, are perfectly satisfied that I have done everything in my power for the service of their commerce ; but what the general opinion of the British Merchants residing here may be, a little time, and their correspondence with their Friends in England will discover more truly than it can be known here upon the spot at present.

Pitt to the Lords of the Admiralty.[1]

WHITEHALL.
MARCH 1ST, 1757.

My LORDS,
I am commanded to signify to your Lordships His Majesty's Pleasure, that you do direct the Captain commanding the Squadron, to be employed in an Expedition to the Coast of Africa, that, in case any Fort or Place shall be taken in those Parts, He should put the same into the Possession of such Officer or Officers of the Marines, as He shall judge proper, leaving the said Officer or Officers there, together with a sufficient number of Marines to keep possession of any such Fort, or Place :   And your Lordships will order such an Additional Number of Marines to be put on board the said Squadron, as you shall think necessary for this purpose.

I am, etc.,
W. PITT.

Pitt to the Duke of Marlborough.[2]

WHITEHALL.
MARCH 1ST, 1757.

My LORD,
His Majesty having thought proper to order a Squadron of Ships of War to proceed on a Secret Expedition to the Coast of Africa ; And it having been represented to the King, that an Engineer will be necessary to attend the same ; I am commanded to signify to your Grace His Majesty's Pleasure, that you do appoint a proper Engineer for this purpose, whom

---

[1] C.O. 267, 12 ; also S. P. Dom. Entry Books, 229, f. 134.
[2] S. P. Dom. Entry Books, 230.

you will direct to repair forthwith to Portsmouth, and there apply to Vice Admiral Boscawen, who will give the necessary Directions for His being received on board, one of His Majesty's Ships to be employed on this Service; And your Grace will direct the said Engineer to follow such orders, as He shall receive from the Commander in Chief of the said Squadron.

I am, etc.,

W. PITT.

Pitt to the Lords of the Admiralty.[1]

WHITEHALL.
JUNE 13TH, 1758.

MY LORDS,

I am commanded to signify to your Lordships His Maj^{tys} Pleasure, that, out of the Transport Vessels, which, by my letter of the 11th post, you were directed to take up, to carry the Regiment of Foot, commanded by Col. Talbot to Jamaica, you do forthwith order such a Number, as shall be sufficient, at the Rate of Two Ton a Man, to receive on board, from the Isle of Wight, Four Companies of the said Regiment, Each Company consisting of Four Commission Officers, Eight non-Commission Officers, Two Drummers, and 100 Private Men, with the usual allowance of Women and Servants; And also 150 Tons of the said Transport Vessels for Ordnance Stores, and Persons belonging to the Artillery, who are to be victualled in the usual manner; And your Lordship will direct the said Transport Vessels, so soon as the Troops and Stores shall be embarked, to proceed, under such Convoy as your Lordships shall think proper, to Fort Lewis on the River Senegal on the Coast of Africa—And it is the King's farther Pleasure, that your Lord^{ps} do, without Loss of Time, cause such an Additional Number of Transport Vessels to be taken up, and properly fitted and victualled, as shall be sufficient, with the remaining Quantity already provided, to carry a Regiment of Foot to Jamaica, agreeable to the Orders contained in my Letter above mentioned of the 11th post.

I am, etc.,

W. PITT.

---

[1] C.O. 267, 12 ; also S. P. Dom. Entry Books, 229.

Pitt to the Secretary at War.[1]

WHITEHALL.
JUNE 13TH, 1758.

MY LORD,

I am commanded to signify to your Lordship His Majesty's Pleasure, that you do forthwith direct Five Companies of the 74th Regiment of Foot, commanded by Colonel Talbot to be compleated to their full Complement of one hundred private men, Rank and File, Each Company, and that the said Four Companies, so compleated, do embark, under the Command of Major Maule, from the Isle of Wight, on board such Transport Vessels, as shall be provided for that purpose by the Lords Commissioners of the Admiralty, and proceed to Fort Lewis on the River Senegal on the Coast of Africa, where the said Troops are to follow such orders, as they shall receive from Major Mason, whom the King has appointed Governor of the said Fort Lewis, and of all other Forts and Places on the River Senegal.

I am, etc.,
W. PITT.

Pitt to Major Mason.[2]

WHITEHALL.
JUNE 15TH, 1758.

MAJOR MASON,

SIR,

Your Letter to the Secretary of the Admiralty, with an account of your Success on the River Senegal, having been laid before His Majesty, I have the Satisfaction to acquaint you, that the King has been pleased entirely to approve your Conduct in the important Service, with which you were entrusted ; And, as the highest Mark thereof, I send you herewith His Majesty's Commission, appointing you Governor of Fort Lewis and of all other Forts and Places, on the Senegal River, of which you should become Master ; And also Commander of His Majesty's Forces that are or shall hereafter be employed on the said River ; together with the Instructions, that the King has been pleased to sign for your Conduct.

---

[1] C.O. 267, 12.   [2] *Ibid.*

As the Preservation and Defence of the Forts and Settlements, of which you are, or may be, in Possession on the River Senegal, are of high Importance to the Trade of these kingdoms, His Majesty has been pleased to order a Reinforcement of Four Hundred Men, Together with a Quantity of Stores and Provisions to be immediately sent to the River Senegal, which, the King hopes will be sufficient to enable you, not only to maintain such Forts and Places as may be already in your Possession on that River ; but also to secure the Fort of Gorée, in case the attempt of Captain Marsh, against that Place, should happily have succeeded. And you will not fail to transmit, by the first Opportunity, the most particular State of the Condition of the Fort and Garrison, and whether you shall judge any farther supplies to be necessary for maintaining the Possession of the said Fort Lewis.

The Season of the Year not admitting of the least Delay in the sending out this Reinforcement, It has not been possible to enter into a Particular Detail of the several Articles, that may be necessary for the Establishment and Settlement of the Trade on the River Senegal ; But His Majesty has been pleased to direct His Servants to take the same under Consideration, and no Time will be lost in sending you such further Orders and Instructions as shall be thought necessary.

I am, etc.,

W. PITT.

Pitt to Governor Mason.[1]

WHITEHALL.
JUNE 21ST, 1758.

SIR,

Mr. Walker having represented the Necessity of a Battery, or Fort, to render the Passage of the Bar, at the Mouth of the River Senegal, impracticable, and secure it against the Inhabitants, I send you inclosed His rough sketch of such a Battery or Fort, as He thinks will best answer these purposes ; And I am commanded to signify to you His Majesty's Pleasure, that you be collecting such materials for building the above Battery or Fort, as are to be found upon the Spot, that the

---

1 C.O. 267, 12.

Plan may be carried into Execution without Loss of Time upon the Arrival of Captain Archer, who is appointed Engineer upon this Service, and will be dispatched for Senegal as soon as possible, with all such necessaries as it may be proper to send from hence, but which could not be got ready in time for this Conveyance.

I am, etc.,
W. PITT.

Pitt to Governor Mason.[1]

WHITEHALL.
JUNE 23RD, 1758.

SIR,

Mr. Saml. Touchet having represented to me, that in consequence of his Engagements with the Lords Commissioners of the Treasury, he now sends Provisions for the Troops at Senegal for four Months, and shall take care to send a further supply before the expiration of that time, and that it will be necessary for this Service, that his Agent Victualler Mr. Saml. Johnson, should have a suitable Apartment for himself and his Clerk, together with proper Storehouses for the Security of the Provisions, and also the use of the small Craft for landing the same ; I am commanded to signify to you His Majesty's Pleasure, that you give the proper directions with regard to the above particulars, and that you take care that Mr. Saml. Johnson has all the assistance necessary, on your part, to enable him to supply the Garrison effectually with Provisions according to his Engagements.

I am, etc.,
W. PITT.

Pitt to the Lords of the Admiralty.[2]

WHITEHALL.
SEPT. 5TH, 1758.

MY LORDS,

I am commanded to signify to your Lordships His Majesty's Pleasure that you do forthwith cause to be provided a quantity of Transport vessels sufficient for 1,000 Persons at

---

[1] C.O. 267, 12.
[2] S. P. Dom. Entry Books, 230.

the rate of Two Tons to each Person, and that the same be victualled for four months and provided with Bedding and other Necessaries, and, having first taken on Board such Troops as shall have Orders to embark at ———— in England, do afterwards proceed under proper Convoy to Cork in Ireland to receive on Board such other Troops as shall have Orders to embark there, and carry them under sufficient convoy to such Place as shall be hereafter directed.

I am, etc.,

W. PITT.

Pitt to the Master-General of the Ordnance.[1]

WHITEHALL.

SEPT. 6TH, 1758.

MY LORD,

His Majesty having thought proper that an Engineer should be forthwith sent to the Island of Senegal on the Coast of Africa and also that an Engineer should be sent to the Island of Jamaica, I am commanded to signify to your Grace His Majesty's Pleasure that you Cause Two Practitioner Engineers to be added to the present Establishment of Engineers, and that your Grace do forthwith appoint a proper Engineer for Senegal, and another for Jamaica, the former must repair immediately to Portsmouth, there to embark on Board of the First of His Majesty's Ships which is to sail for Senegal of which upon application to the Lords Commissioners of the Admiralty, he will be more particularly informed, and the latter must repair to Jamaica, the first convenient opportunity.

I am, etc.,

W. PITT.

Pitt to the Master-General of the Ordnance.[2]

WHITEHALL,

SEPT. 9TH, 1758.

MY LORD,

I am commanded to signify to your grace, His Majesty's Pleasure, that you do forthwith give Directions for embarking on Board such Transports, as you shall order to be

---

[1] S. P. Dom. Entry Books, 230.   [2] *Ibid.*

immediately taken and properly fitted for that Purpose, Heavy
Brass Ordnance compleat 9 Pounders, 8, with 200 Rounds of
round Shot and 50 Rounds of Grape Shot to each ; also Brass
Mortars compleat 8 Inches, 6, with 150 Rounds of Shells to
each, also two Petards compleat, with a just Proportion of
Stores, Artificers and Attendants the whole to Proceed as
soon as possible upon Foreign Service, under such convoy
as the Lords of the Admiralty shall appoint.

I am, etc.,

W. PITT.

Pitt to the Lords of the Admiralty. [1]

WHITEHALL.
SEPT. 30TH, 1758.

MY LORDS,

I am commanded to signify to your Lordships His
Majesty's pleasure, that you do direct a Squadron of the King's
Ships ; consisti g of five Ships of the Line, two Bomb vessels,
and a proper Number of Frigates to be prepared for foreign
service, and that the said Squadron be put under the Com-
mand of the Honble Augustus Keppel, whom your Lordships
will direct to follow such orders, as he shall receive from His
Majesty by one of His Principal Secretaries of State ; and
Your Lordships will further direct the Transports for 1,000
Persons, which were ordered by my letter of the 5th Inst., having
first taken on Board at Portsmouth 200 Draughts from the
Sixty Sixth Regiment of Foot, to proceed forthwith, under
such Convoy of such part of Mr. Keppel's Squadron, as Your
Lordships shall judge proper, to Cork, where they are to receive
on board the 2nd Battalion of the Seventy Sixth Regiment
of Foot after which the said Transports, with all the Troops
above mentioned on board, are to follow such Directions as
they shall receive from Capt. Keppel, for their future proceedings.

I am, etc.,

W. PITT.

---

[1] S. P. Dom. Entry Books, 230.

Pitt to the Secretary at War. [1]

WHITEHALL.
OCT. 2ND, 1758.

MY LORD,

In my letter of the 21st August, I signified to your Lordship, the King's pleasure, that a Draft of 200 Men should be made from Col. La Fausille's Regiment of Foot for North America; I am now to signify to you, It is His Majesty's pleasure that you do give the necessary directions that the draft of 200 Men from the said Regiment now at Southampton, do embark on board such Transport vessels as shall be appointed by the Lords Commissioners of the Admiralty to receive them, and proceed under the direction of Commodore Keppel to Ireland, where they are to await (without disembarking) such orders for their future proceedings, as they shall there receive.

I am, etc.,
W. PITT.

Pitt to the Master-General of the Ordnance. [2]

WHITEHALL.
OCT. 4TH, 1758.

MY LORD,

Having in my Letter of the 6th post, signified to your Grace His Majesty's Pleasure that an Engineer should be sent to Senegal, on the Coast of Africa; and also, in my Letter of the 9th post, signified His Majesty's farther pleasure that a train, therein specified, together with a just proportion of Ordnance Stores and with the Artificers and attendants necessary, should be embarked on board Transports, to be taken up, by your Grace for that purpose, to proceed, as soon as possible, upon foreign Service; I am now to inform your Grace, that it is the King's Pleasure that the Transports having on board the above Engineer, Train, etc., be immediately put under the command of Captain Keppel.

I am, etc,
W. PITT.

---

[1] S. P. Dom. Entry Books, 230.
[2] *Ibid.*

Pitt to the Master-General of the Ordnance.[1]

WHITEHALL.
OCT. 9TH, 1758.

MY LORD,

I am commanded to signify to your Grace His Majesty's Pleasure, that you do forthwith direct the Engineer who is to serve in the Expedition under the Command of Capt. Keppel to repair to Portsmouth ; Your Grace will also direct the proper Officer at Portsmouth to supply Mr. Keppel's Squadron with such a number of Royals, out of those now at that place, as may be spared, without prejudice to the other foreign Service already ordered and which is to take place forthwith. And your Grace will likewise order Mr. Keppel's Squadron to be furnished with such a Number of Working Tools, as he shall think necessary.

I am, etc.,
W. PITT.

Pitt to the Lords of the Admiralty.[2]

WHITEHALL.
OCT. 10TH, 1758.

MY LORDS,

Having rec^d. information from the Board of Ordnance, that the Transport called the *Pretty Betsy*, loaded with Ordnance Stores, intended for foreign Service has suffered considerably in the late hard Gale of Wind, and that the said Transport can't proceed upon the service for which she is destined without being refitted, I am commanded to signify to your Lordships His Majesty's Pleasure, that you do forthwith give the necessary Orders to the proper person in His Majesty's Yard at Sheerness to give all possible assistance for refitting the above Transport, and as soon as she is again fit for the sea, your Lordships will give orders for her sailing under proper Convoy to Portsmouth without loss of time.

I am, etc.,
W. PITT.

---

[1] S. P. Dom. Entry Books, 230, f. 23.
[2] *Ibid.*, f. 21.

Pitt to the Secretary at War.[1]

WHITEHALL.
OCT. 16TH, 1758.

MY LORD,

The King having thought proper that the Second Battalion of the 76th Regiment of Foot commanded by Lord Forbes should be ordered to embark immediately at Cork in Ireland, to proceed upon foreign Service, I am to inform your Lordship, that such orders are given, that your Lordship may give such directions as you shall judge proper with regard to the said Battalion.

I am, etc.,
W. PITT.

Pitt to Captain Keppel.[2]

WHITEHALL.
OCT. 17TH, 1758.

SIR,

I have received the Favor of your Letter of the 15th Instant, giving an Account, that, you hoped, the Squadron, under your Command, would be ready to sail as this Day; but that the Repair of the Damages of the Ordnance ship will not be compleated by that Time, and therefore you were desirous of Directions concerning Her; I am to signify to you the King's Pleasure, that you do not defer your Sailing One Moment on Account of the said Ordnance Ship, but that you do leave Her at Portsmouth, with Orders to sail for Her Destination, as soon as she shall be ready, with all possible Expedition, under such Convoy as the Lords of the Admiralty shall direct.

I am, etc.,
W. PITT.

Pitt to the Lords of the Admiralty.[3]

WHITEHALL.
OCT. 18TH, 1758.

MY LORDS,

Captain Keppel having acquainted me, that the ordnance Ship now at Portsmouth, repairing some damages

---

[1] S. P. Dom. Entry Books, 230.   [2] C.O. 267, 12.
[3] S. P. Dom. Entry Books, 230, f. 31.

which she received in the late high Winds, would not be compleated by the Time the Squadron under his Command would
be ready ; His Majesty was pleased to command me to direct
Mr. Keppel not to defer his sailing one moment, on account
of the said Ordnance Ship, and I send Your Lordships inclosed
a Copy of my Letter to Captain Keppel, on this Subject, in
order that your Lordships may forthwith direct such Convoy as
you shall think proper to proceed with the Ordnance Ship ——
above mentioned to her Destination, as soon as she shall be
ready, in Case she shall not sail at the same time as Mr. Keppel.

I am, etc.,

W. PITT.

Pitt to the Lords of the Admiralty.[1]

WHITEHALL.
JULY 31ST, 1759.

My Lords,

I am commanded to signify to your Lordships His
Majesty's Pleasure, that, out of such part of the Transport
vessels, ordered by my Letter of April 17th and May 16th, as
are now at Spithead, you do forthwith cause a sufficient number
to be fitted up for the reception of five hundred Men, at the
rate of Two Tons for each Person, and that the same be victualled for Four Months whole allowance for the above number
of Men, and provided with all other necessaries for foreign
Service.

I am, etc.,

W. PITT.

Pitt to the Lords of the Admiralty.

WHITEHALL.
AUG. 9TH, 1759.

My Lords,

I am commanded to signify to your Lordships His
Majesty's Pleasure, that you do give the necessary Orders for
400 Men, with the proper Officers to command them, to be
embarked at Portsmouth, with all possible Expedition, on board
the Transport Vessels, ordered by my Letter of the 31st post,
to be fitted up and provided with all necessaries, for foreign

---

[1] S. P. Dom. Entry Books, 230, f. 54.   [2] C.O. 267, 12.

Service; And your Lordships will direct the said Transport Vessels, with the Troops on board, to proceed without Loss of Time, under such Convoy as your Lordships shall judge proper, to the Coast of Africa, where Part of the said Men are to be disembarked at Fort Lewis in the River Senegal, and the Rest, at the Island of Gorée, agreeably to the Orders which Gov. Worge, or the Commander of His Majesty's Forces in Africa, shall receive for that Purpose.

I am, etc.,

W. PITT.

P.S.—Your Lordships will be pleased to forward the inclosed Letter to Gov. Worge at Senegal.

Pitt to the Secretary at War.[1]

WHITEHALL.
AUG. 9TH, 1759.

My Lord,

The King having judged it expedient, that a Reinforcement should be forthwith sent to His Garrison at Fort Lewis in the River Senegal, and at the Island of Gorée, I am to signify His Majesty's Pleasure to your Lordship, that you do forthwith cause a Draught of 100 Men, with proper officers to command them, to be made from each of the four following Regiments of Foot, viz. the 67th, 69th, and 72nd, and 75th. And that you do direct the said 400 Men, so draughted with the officers, to embark at Portsmouth, with all possible Expedition; on board such Transport Vessels, as the Lords Commissioners of the Admiralty are directed to provide for their Reception, and to carry them to the Coast of Africa; where 200 of the said Men are to be disembarked at Fort Lewis in the River Senegal, and the other 200 at Gorée, unless Govr. Worge, or the Commander of His Majesty's Forces in Africa, shall from Circumstances on the Spot, which cannot be known here, find the above Distribution of the 400 Men impracticable, or shall judge it absolutely necessary for the King's Service, to make some alteration in the said Disposition; And your Lordship will accordingly dispatch to the Commanding

---

[1] C.O. 267, 12.

Officers at Fort Lewis, and at Gorée, such orders, as shall be
necessary for the Reception and Distribution of the above
Reinforcements, agreeably to the Contents of this Letter.

I am, etc.,

W. PITT.

S.P.F. Venice 67.

Pitt to Consul John Murray.

WHITEHALL.

NOV. 29TH, 1757.

MR. MURRAY,

SIR,

The inclosed papers will fully inform you of the State
of a Demand of Messrs. Brown, Woodbridge and Woodmass,
Merchants of London, upon Captain Wilford, Master of the
ship called *Nevis Planter* (which name he has since changed
to the *Fuller*) now at Venice and of the great reason they have
to apprehend, from his irregular proceedings ever since he left
England that he will attempt to evade the payment of what is
justly due to them, by setting up, in the name of his children,
the same claim, of which he has availed himself with regard
to a further sum of money he had taken up of Consul Smith
at Venice. But you will observe that it is the opinion of Mr.
Pratt, His Majesty's Attorney General, that however the
particular law of Venice may be deemed to affect a Transaction at that place, there can be no pretence that it should take
place against an agreement made in London, between His
Majesty's Subjects only ; It is therefore the King's Pleasure,
that you do take all proper and legal methods to prevent the
effect of any such attempt on the part of Captain Wilford ;
and His Majesty is persuaded the known justice of the Republick of Venice, that when this case is represented to them
in its true light, they will suffer the Law of England to take
place, and not give any countenance to such proceedings of
Captain Wilford in order to defraud his creditors of their just
demands which would undoubtedly have very ill Consequences
with regard to trade, by lessening that security which has always
been held so valid, for money taken up by the Master of a ship.

I am, etc.,

W. PITT.

S.P.F. Portugal 50.

Translation of a letter from the Prime Minister [1] *at Lisbon to one of the chief managers of the Wine Co. at Oporto, Dec.*5, 1756.

EXTRACTS DEALING WITH THE OBJECTIONS OF SOME OF THE PORTUGUESE MERCHANTS TO THE COMPANY.

But there is the Errour of these miserable, ignorant perverse wretches, in not considering that every one must conform to the will of their king and not act contrary.

. . . . .

Tell them that they should take notice of the hatred the English has to the Company and judge what is the cause; If it is against the Portuguese, what does it concern the English whether it be for our good or not; but it is their having better knowledge and Intelligence of trade, I know the mark they aim at, which is to Inrich themselves by draining from us their unjust gains, by our ignorance and negligence they make themselves masters of our commerce as well in this kingdom as in the Brazils, sucking out all our Blood and we like statues of stone insensible of feeling, altho our Royal Physician finding such desperate symptoms has applyed frequent remedies and yet we don't feel them, so that they continue making all to their advantage and we not to submit to such a King who studies how to make us Happy confirms evidently what they say of us, that our Kingdom is a century behind other nations.

S.P.F. Portugal 51.

Pitt to Hay, Consul at Lisbon.

WHITEHALL.
SEPT. 5TH, 1758.

SIR,

Some of the Merchants Trading to Portugal, having lately delivered to me a very strong memorial representing the detriment, that, they conceive must arise to their trade from the Establishment of the new Wine Co. at Oporto, which they alledge to be, in many respects contrary to the treaties subsisting with the crown of Portugal, particularly with regard

---

[1] Pombal.

to the rights and Privileges of the Judge Conservator ; I send you the enclosed a copy of the said memorial, and as you are so perfectly master of this subject I desire when you shall have duly considered this Piece and the facts therein alledged that you would transmit to me your thoughts thereupon and how far this Co. may really affect the British trade, or be at all contrary to treaty and in case any mitigations, or considerations should appear to be essentially necessary to render the new Regulations more conformable to treaties and to the established Privileges of the British Merchants, you may as from yourself, endeavour to sound Mr. Dacuntia, in what manner any application on this subject might be received, mixing at the same time, the warmest assurances of the King's cordial Friendship and of his firm Reliance on His Most Faithful Majesty's Just and Favourable Intentions, but you are not on any account to make use of His Majesty's Name on this particular matter, or appear to have received any directions on the Subject.

I am, etc.,

W. PITT.

Credential for Thomas Cumming.[1]

George, the Second, by the Grace of God, King of Great Britain, France and Ireland, Defender of the Christian Faith, etc., Duke of Brunswick and Lunenburg, Arch Treasurer and Prince Elector of the Holy Roman Empire, etc. To the High and Glorious Monarch, the Mighty and Right Noble Prince Amir Sultan, King of Legibbilli, Greeting. High and Glorious Monarch Our Trusty Subject, Thomas Cumming, who will deliver this Letter to your Majesty, having made a Faithfull Report of the Friendship you have expressed for us, We take this first opportunity of assuring your Majesty of the Great Regard we have for your Person, and Our Desire to show you, on Our Part, all possible Marks of Friendship and Esteem, as a Proof of which We have Ordered a Number of Our Great Ships of War to repair to your Dominions, and assist such Forces, as your Majesty shall employ in reducing the Forts and Settlements, that have been unjustly erected by our Common and Perfidious Enemy the French, on the River Senegal, or elsewhere, on the Frontiers of your Dominions, and We have directed

---

[1] C.O. 267, 12, endorsed "Drat. to African King, Feb. 1, 1757."

our said Subject, Thomas Cumming, to whom We desire Your Majesty would give entire Credence, to explain more particularly to your Majesty Our Royal Intentions in sending the said Ships of War, the Commander of which will be presented to you by the said Thomas Cumming, and We do not doubt but the said Commander will act in such a manner as shall be agreeable to your Majesty, and that He will be ready to give you all the assistance in the Execution of your Designs against our Common Enemy, the French as shall be proper and convenient for our said Ships to undertake. We wish your Majesty all true Happiness, Health, and Prosperity, and recommend you to the Protection of Almighty God. Given at Our Palace at St. James's the First Day of February in the year of our Lord 1757 and of Our Reign the Thirtieth.

Your most affectionate Friend,

GEORGE R.

W. PITT.

S.P.F. Denmark 105.

Private and Secret.

COPENHAGEN.
MAY 29TH, 1759.

MY LORD,

Baron Bernstorff has desired me to insinuate privately to your Lordship, that the King, Our Royal Master, will probably soon have in His Power an easy opportunity of conferring a particular obligation upon the Great Duchess of Russia. The case is this, Baron Wolfe, His Majesty's Consul General in that Country being now so ill, that His Decease may justly be expected, Her Royal Highness, when the Post becomes vacant, would be extremely glad to see it filled by Mr. Wroughton, an English Merchant at Petersburg. So that if His Majesty pleases to distinguish the said Mr. Wroughton, by chusing Him when proposed by his Consul General in Russia, M. de Bernstorff assures me (upon the authority of a letter from M. de Oste the Danish Minister at the Russian Court) that nothing can be more agreeable to that Princess, who will take it as a singular Favour at His Majesty's hands. However, as M. Wolfe, they say is endeavouring to secure the Reversion of His Employment for a Kinsman of His Own, the Grand

P

Duchess would by no means appear to thwart His View, and therefore earnestly desires, this application may remain a Secret.

I am with all Duty and Respect My Lord,
Your Lordship's
Most humble and most obedient servant,
WALTER TITLEY

Pitt to Governor Worge.[1]

WHITEHALL.
AUG. 9TH, 1759.

GOVERNOR WORGE,
SIR,

I have received and laid before the King your Letters of the 2nd February, and 24th March, such parts whereof as related to Provisions for the Garrison under your Command, and to Presents and Customs, to the Natives, and other matters of Expence were immediately transmitted to the Treasury that the necessary Directions might be given thereupon ; And I am informed by the Duke of Newcastle, that a Quantity of Goods, proper for Presents to the Natives, will be sent out by this Conveyance, and that the particular Distribution thereof is entrusted to your Judgement on the Spot, His Majesty relying on your Prudence and Discretion, that you will dispose of the same in such manner, as shall best answer the purpose of preserving the Natives in their alliance with, and Dependence on the King, and that you will be careful to avoid any Expence that shall not be necessary.

I am now to acquaint you, that His Majesty having received Information that the French may meditate some attempt to repossess themselves of Senegal or Gorée, and, most probably of both those Places, has judged it expedient to order a Reinforcement of 400 Men to be sent, with all possible Expedition, for the Garrisons of both the above Places, vizt., Fort Lewis in the River Senegal, and Gorée, and you will receive from the Secretary at War, the necessary Orders with regard to the particular Distribution of the said 400 Men, between the two Garrisons above mentioned.

I am, etc.,
W. PITT.

---

[1] C.O. 267, 12.

Pitt to Govr. Worge.[1]

WHITEHALL.
MARCH 15TH, 1759.

GOVR. WORGE,

SIR,

I have been favoured with your Letters of the 1st and 17th January, the Former giving an Account of the Success of His Majesty's Arms against Gorée; and tho' the ill behaviour of the Enemy did not afford the Land Forces under your Command, any opportunity to distinguish themselves on that Occasion, yet, the King does not doubt, from the Readiness and Ardor they shewed, they would have performed their Duty in such manner, as would have supported His Majesty's Arms.

With regard to your other Letter, containing an Account of your Arrival at Fort Lewis, on the River Senegal, in order to your taking upon you the Government of that place; I am to acquaint you, that the King was sorry to hear that there was any variance between the Garrison and the Inhabitants; and His Majesty entirely approves your Intention to endeavour to reconcile them by amicable means, It being the King's Pleasure, that you should use all proper Measures in your Power to cultivate, and improve the Friendship of any of the Natives, who may have shewed an Inclination to live in good Harmony with the English, and to carry on Trade with them; you will also use all possible means to induce any of the Natives, who may have still any attachment for the French, to come over, and submit themselves; And any reasonable and necessary sum, that you shall expend, in Presents, for the above purposes, will be repaid you.

I am to signify to you the King's further Pleasure that you should carefully endeavour to discover the Nature of the Trade, which the French have carried on, up the River Senegal, as well as the Various Productions, and Sources of the Riches, of those Countries; and I am particularly to recommend it to you to give all the assistance in your Power to any Person who shall be sent to the Places within your Government, by the Company of Merchants Trading to Africa, to enquire into the nature of the Gum, and other Trades. And you will not fail to give equally and impartially, all possible Assistance and

---

[1] C.O. 267, 12.

Protection to all His Majesty's Subjects who may come, on
Account of Trade, to Fort Lewis, or other Forts or Places under
your Government.

I am, etc.,

W. PITT.

List of Artillery, and Stores, and proper Persons to attend
the same, on an Expedition to the Coast of Africa.[1]

No.

Light Brass Ordnance ⎫	12 Pounders -	-	-	4
with Carriages Compleat ⎬	6 Pounders -	-	-	6

Brass Mortars with Beds ⎫	$5\frac{1}{2}$ inch -	-	-	8
compleat ⎬				

With 200 Rounds of Round Shot fixed, and 50 Rounds of Tin
Cased Shot fixed for each of the Guns, and 100 Rounds of
Shells for each of the Mortars, with a Necessary Proportion
of Stores to accompany the same.   Likewise

Hand granadoes fixed	-	-	-	-	-	1200
Scaling Ladders of 30 ft.	-	-	-	-	-	24
Intrenching Tools for 300 Men.					

With the following Persons to attend the same :

    1 Engineer.
    1 Clerk of Stores.
    1 Conductor.
    1 Carpenter.
    1 Smith.

Sand Bags ⎰Bushel	-	-	-	-	500
⎱$\frac{1}{2}$ Bushel	-	-	-	-	2000

20 Wall Pieces.

A Detachment from the Royal Regiment of Artillery, consisting of Two Officers, and Twenty-five Men.

Pitt to the Lords of the Admiralty.

WHITEHALL.

JAN. 12TH, 1758.

MY LORDS,
    I am commanded to signify to Your Lordships His
Majesty's Pleasure that you do direct Two Ships of the Line,

---

[1] Endorsed, " Sent to the Ordnance, Jan. 12, 1758."
[2] C.O. 267, 12, endorsed " Drat. to the Lords of the Admiralty,
Jan. 12, 1758, Africa."

One Frigate, One Sloop, and Two Busses, or such other Vessels as Your Lordships shall judge most proper, to be prepared for a Secret Expedition to the River Senegal on the Coast of Africa, and to proceed forthwith on that Service ; And that you do cause Two Hundred Marines, with proper Commission, and Non-Commission, Officers, over and above the full Complements of the said Ships to be embarked on board the Same ; And His Majesty having ordered for this Service a certain Proportion of Artillery and Stores, together with an Engineer and other proper Persons to attend the Same, Your Lordships will give the necessary Directions for the said Artillery, Stores, and Persons, to be received on board the Ships, that you shall order for that purpose ; And Your Lordships will direct the Commander of the Ships, employed on this Expedition, to land, if He shall find it practicable, the Two Hundred Marines or any Part of them, Together with the Artillery, under the Command of such Officer of the Marines, as Your Lordships shall appoint to command the same, when so landed, in order to attack, if it shall be judged practicable, any French Fort or Forts, and Settlements, on the River Senegal on the Coast of Africa, or to annoy the Enemy in any other manner, that shall be found most effectual ; and Your Lordships will direct the Commander of the Ships to give all necessary and proper assistance, as far as shall be consistent with the safety of His Majesty's Ships, in the Execution of the above Service ; And in case any French Fort or Forts shall be taken, It is the King's Pleasure that the whole, or a sufficient Number of the said Two Hundred Marines under the Command of such Marine Officer as Your Lordships shall appoint together with such ships as shall be necessary for that purpose do remain, and keep Possession of the said Fort or Forts until they shall receive the King's further Orders ; But in Case it shall not be judged advisable to keep Possession of such Fort or Forts, Your Lordships will order the same to be effectually demolished.

It is also the King's further Pleasure, that Your Lordships do cause a sufficient Quantity of Provisions to be put on board the Ships above mentioned, not only for the subsistance of Two Hundred Marines and the Persons belonging to the Artillery, during their Passage, and the Stay of the Ships, on the Coast of Africa, but also for the Support of such Men, as may

remain there to keep Possession of any Fort, and Your Lordships will accordingly direct such provisions, as shall be
necessary for this purpose, to be landed and left with the
Men.

I am, etc.,

W. PITT.

Pitt to the Master-General of the Ordnance. [1]

WHITEHALL.

JAN. 12TH, 1758.

MY LORD,

The King having been pleased to order a Squadron
of Ships of War to proceed on an Expedition to the Coast of
Africa, I am commanded to signify to your Grace His Majesty's
Pleasure, that you do appoint a proper Engineer for that
Service together with the Artillery and Ordnance Stores, etc.,
specified in the List hereto annexed ; and you will direct the
said Engineer to apply to Lord Anson, who will give orders
for his being received on Board one of His Majesty's Ships
employed on this Expedition.

I am, etc.,

W. PITT.

---

[1] C.O. 267, 12.

INDEX

Q